The
Mayflower
Hotel

The Mayflower Hotel

Grande Dame of Washington, D.C.

by Judith R. Cohen

BALANCE HOUSE, LTD.
NEW YORK

ACKNOWLEDGMENTS

I deeply appreciate the gracious cooperation of the following:

Dominic Antonelli, Ulysses Auger, Richard Cohen, and Kingdon Gould, Jr., all of whom gave freely of their time; Sylvia Rivchun, whose contribution in research and editing was invaluable; Mark Gabor for his skillful editorial assistance; Roxanne Deane and Victor Dyni of the Martin Luther King, Jr. Library; Frances Heffler; James Massey; Hope Ridings Miller; and Myrna Statland. My gratitude also to Mayflower people old and new: Bernard Awenenti, Bob Beaver, William Cook, Eddie Derendorf, Virginia Falta-Lee, Pete Flaherty, Beverly Glaine, Frank Glaine, Jean Herring, William Hulett, Donald James, the later Milton Kronheim, Marilyn Piety, Burt Pisapia, Reginald Redmond, Sidney Seidenman, Jr., Angelo Stavropoulos, Jocko Tutela, Lawrence Wiesinger; and Virginia Washburne; and to all the many others who contributed in some way to making this book a reality.

The historical pictures in these pages were obtained from many sources, particularly the collection of Michael Jarboe and the files of photographers John Di Joseph and Arthur Rosen.

The color photographs were all taken especially for this book by Daniel Kramer, except for the photos of the wedding ceremony, the wedding reception, and the buffet table, which were taken by Monte Zucker, and the photo of Mr. and Mrs. Walter Washington, which was taken by Harry Naltchayan.

J.R.C.

Copyright © 1987 by Judith R. Cohen.

All Rights Reserved. No part of this book may be reproduced or transmitted in any form or by any means, electronic or mechanical, including photocopy, recording or any information storage and retrieval system, without permission in writing from the publisher.

Library of Congress Cataloging-in-Publication Data

Cohen, Judith R., 1941-
   The Mayflower Hotel : grande dame of Washington, D.C. / by Judith R. Cohen.
       p.   cm.
   ISBN 0–940577–00–3 : $29.95
   1. Mayflower Hotel (Washington, D.C.)   I. Title.
TX941.M39C64 1987
647'.9475301—dca2 —dc19   87-18428
                                                                  CIP

Printed in Italy by Amilcare Pizzi, S.p.A.

PUBLISHER'S NOTE

Many of the people named in this book have changed their positions or titles over the years—e.g., President Kennedy was formerly Senator Kennedy—and usually the text refers to "then Senator" or "former Senator", etc. Whether or not such a designation is used, it should be understood that the title given is always the one held at the time of the occasion described or illustrated.

The black-and-white photographs are illustrations of The Mayflower's past and are located in appropriate places in the story. The color photographs show The Mayflower since its restoration and appear throughout the book without reference to the historical text.

This book is dedicated to my mother, Lillian Rosen Ratner, who taught me the meaning of Love, and to the most important men in my life: Philip Rosen, my father, who through the many happy hours spent with me telling wonderful stories, gave me the love of learning and the confidence to fulfill my dreams; William Cohen, my father-in-law, whose unconditional love, great sense of humor, and appreciation of life are a constant inspiration; and most of all, Richard Cohen, my husband, without whose loving support, understanding, and encouragement, this book would never have happened.

Contents

CHAPTER ONE

Introducing a Washington Landmark

$\mathcal{The}$ *grande dame* of Connecticut Avenue is looking her very best again. Not since she first opened her doors in 1925 has The Mayflower appeared so opulent and elegant. A face lift and a new wardrobe have removed the wear and tear of the last six decades—but none of her charm and history.

Through her doors have come all the U.S. Presidents since Calvin Coolidge, heads of state from every continent, members of Congress and the Supreme Court, diplomats, captains of industry, Broadway and Hollywood stars, artists, debutantes, dowagers, and tourists from the world over.

It was in The Mayflower that Charles Lindbergh celebrated his historic flight, Winston Churchill sat for his portrait, Will Rogers quipped for members of Congress, the Duke and Duchess of Windsor enjoyed a cup of coffee, and a delegation of Chinese diplomats from the walled-in Mainland occupied a block of rooms for over eight months.

This photo of Lindbergh appeared in the June 1927 edition of the Mayflower's magazine Rudder *as "The first posed photograph of Colonel Charles A. Lindbergh upon his return to America—Posed in the Chinese Room of the Mayflower". Following a breakfast reception on June 13,* Rudder *reported Lindbergh's departure from Washington: ". . . he made a vertical ascent from the field that caused veteran airmen to gasp. After 'stunting' over the Potomac awhile, Lindy swept away to New York where he was greeted with the greatest reception ever accorded an individual anywhere".*

Political humorist Will Rogers was a frequent guest at the hotel. He is shown here at a live radio broadcast from the Grand Ballroom, c. 1931.

J. Edgar Hoover was a Mayflower regular, eating the same lunch at the same table for twenty years. Harry Truman thought of The Mayflower as his home away from home. Long before security became a presidential imperative, he would stroll up Connecticut Avenue to the hotel to get his shoes shined or to drop in on a personal friend or two.

The Mayflower has been a place to celebrate, to conduct business, to negotiate, to create, to dine, to sleep, and to live. It has been a stamping ground for generations of entertainers. Appearing as either guests or performers were an impressive array of celebrities: Al Jolson, Tallulah Bankhead, Jean Harlow, Myrna Loy, Bette Davis, Lauren Bacall, Jean Arthur, Helen Hayes, Spencer Tracy, James Cagney, Amos 'n' Andy, John Wayne, Edgar Bergen and Charlie McCarthy, Danny Kaye, Red Skelton, Mickey Rooney, Andy Griffith, Ginger Rogers, Broderick Crawford, Rex Harrison, Kim Novak, Arthur Godfrey, Bob Hope, Mary Martin, Pat Boone, Ethel Merman, Carol Channing, Robert Goulet, Raymond Burr, Marlon Brando, Frank Sinatra, Diana Ross, and scores of others.

During the Depression, according to The Mayflower's Log, *"The world's favorite motion picture stars, Mary Pickford and Doug Fairbanks" stayed at The Mayflower while visiting Washington "in the interest of benefit motion-picture performances that are being staged throughout the country to aid the unemployed".*

Bob Hope with Banquet Manager Walter Seligman in front of one of the James Tyler paintings of the ship Mayflower.

Claudette Colbert

Olivia De Havilland

Erroll Flynn, chatting with Democratic
Committee Chairman Ed Flynn

*Photographs
by Dulaney
and Warner Bros.*

Hollywood
at the
Mayflower

■ Army and Navy Relief benefits and the War
Bond campaign are the powerful magnets which
have lured many of movieland's brightest stars to
Washington in recent weeks. As the list of Hollywood visitors grows, one begins to wonder who is
left in California to make the movies!

Paulette Goddard

Groucho Marx

Dorothy Lamour, with
Presidential Secretary
Marvin McIntyre

A page from The Mayflower's Log *during World War II,
featuring movie stars who attended the Mayflower's Army
and Navy Relief benefits.*

Gloria Swanson poses with a marble statue of Hiawatha at the entrance to The Mayflower Lounge.

Hollywood producer Cecil B. DeMille (right) at the hotel with his private pilot, Paul Mantz.

President Roosevelt was unable to attend his own birthday celebration in 1943, but many celebrities turned up at the several Mayflower functions: (left to right) Robert Young with the Vice-President's wife, Mrs. Henry Wallace; England's Foreign Minister, Lord Halifax, with actresses Janet Blair and Laraine Day; a very young Roddy McDowall looking up to Loretta Young and Edgar Bergen at a reception in the Chinese Room. At right, James Cagney with the Mayflower's general manager, C. J. Mack.

Edgar Bergen and friend Charlie McCarthy preparing to perform at Franklin Delano Roosevelt's 61st birthday party.

A smiling Al Jolson, in the Mayflower lobby, as Master of Ceremonies at FDR's 1943 birthday ball.

Alan Ladd.

*Actor James Stewart at FDR's
1943 birthday celebration.*

*Mr. and Mrs. Douglas Fairbanks,
Jr. attend a benefit at The Mayflower.*

*Rex Harrison and Lili Palmer
(Mrs. Rex Harrison) shown here
with Hazel Markel, one-time
president of The Women's National Press Club and a radio
personality.*

Mary Pickford.

Marge and Gower Champion, 1955.

Mary Martin.

William Bendix with Coast Guard Admiral Joseph F. Farley.

Eva Gabor checking in.

Danny Thomas poses for the camera on October 21, 1961.

A special guest of The Mayflower was the cheetah movie star Hitari, here being served in the hotel's elegant style.

Above, one of a pair of bronze statues in the Cafe Promenade.

At right, one of the Mayflower's two monumental antique Sèvres vases.

Amelia Earhart Putnam, famed aviatrix, stayed at The Mayflower when she received the Special Gold Medal of the National Geographic Society for her solo flight across the Atlantic.

Mr. and Mrs. Andy Griffith with journalist David Brinkley and Mrs. Fred A. Morrison.

Charles Coburn, Alexis Smith, and Caesar Romero at a reception in the hotel.

Also peopling The Mayflower were foreign dignitaries from all the continents—among them Mohammad Reza Pahlavi (the Shah of Iran), President Charles de Gaulle of France, King Saud of Saudi Arabia, Prince Takamatsu of Japan, Prince (later King) Olaf and Princess Martha of Norway, King Peter of Yugoslavia, Chancellor Konrad Adenauer of West Germany, President Rafael Trujillo of the Dominican Republic, Anwar Sadat of Egypt, and Emperor Haile Selassie of Ethiopia.

Its attractiveness to outsiders notwithstanding, The Mayflower has also been a magnet for the party givers and party goers of Washington. For more than six decades, whenever Washingtonians wanted a grand affair they thought of The Mayflower. Thousands of brides cut their wedding cakes in the Grand Ballroom, hundreds of debutantes made their formal bows, scores of babies received their first official blessings, and relationships too numerous to count have been created and cemented at luncheons, dinner parties, graduations, bar mitzvahs, tea dances, charity balls, cocktail parties, and other private celebrations.

Often the Mayflower's parties entailed major redecorating of the Ballroom to simulate exotic places and atmospheres with the appropriate trappings—a sultan's palace, for example, or a circus with live animals, or a replica of New York's infamous discotheque, Studio 54. There was once an evening when the Ballroom was tented in pink chiffon and decorated to look like a Renaissance painting. Unplucked ducks and pheasants were laid out on a table, along with wild turkeys, geese, and several varieties of game chicken. The three hundred guests were serenaded by ten violinists and fêted with foods as varied as caviar crêpes, spinach gnocchi, and marzipan.

The Mayflower started its voyage through history with a regal christening—chandeliers aglitter, Oriental

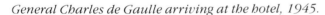

General Charles de Gaulle arriving at the hotel, 1945.

View of the Promenade looking west toward the main entrance on Connecticut Avenue.

The Promenade at Christmas, showing the annual Special Olympics Christmas trees. Decorated by some of Washington's finest department stores and interior decorators, these trees are sold at auction to benefit the Special Olympics Fund.

*Debutantes lined up at the Mayflower's glamorous Black and White Ball, late 1920s.
(below) Washington bachelors pass along the receiving line at the Ball.*

carpets unfurled, gold-decked columns sparkling, and the world's elite chatting, laughing, and dancing through its halls. In subsequent years the hotel changed hands twice, and each time some of its most striking features disappeared. Two enormous skylights were blacked out during World War II, for fear of air raids. Other changes were made in the name of modernism. The hotel's 24-karat-gold trim was painted over, the marble pillars in the lobby were covered by wood paneling, the mezzanine disappeared behind a dropped ceiling (to add office space), splendid murals were lost, and solid bronze doors gave way to stainless steel and glass.

In 1966 The Mayflower was purchased by a group of local investors who decided to restore the hotel to its original grandeur. At a cost of $65 million, The Mayflower in 1985 again became what it once was—a traditional grand hotel, with completely refurbished rooms and suites, regilded lobbies and ballrooms, reopened skylights. In addition, there are new restaurants and kitchen facilities, and completely modernized plumbing, heating, and electricity.

It cost more to restore the hotel than it cost to build it originally. But the restoration was worth the price: It earned The Mayflower its rightful place on the National Register of Historic Places, and it has regained the hotel's earlier reputation as "the second best address in Washington".

The renovated Mayflower, with 648 rooms and 76 suites, is serviced by more than five hundred employees. Half of the staff have been with the hotel for ten years or more, and some have been members of the Mayflower family for almost half a century.

The hotel has entered a new era. But its present course is the same one that was set in 1925. The Mayflower is not the only first-class hotel in Washington today, but it is inextricably bound up with the history of the nation's capital and—in many ways—of the nation itself.

The receiving line at the 1985 debutante Christmas Ball. According to The Washingtonian *magazine (March 1986), "When the time comes, the girls are presented to the company one by one. Each girl slips gracefully through the shrubbery off the loggia on the arm of her papa—or, even better, her grandfather—and makes a modest curtsy."*

The Hair Salon.

Entrance to the Cafe Promenade, with seventeenth-century Aubusson tapestry at right.

The Town and Country Lounge.

The central meeting area for thirteen private conference rooms on the second floor. Each of the rooms is named for one of America's original thirteen colonies.

*The 1960 state banquet for Their Majesties King Bhumibol
Adulyadej and Queen Sirikit of Thailand, held in the
Grand Ballroom.*

*Archduke Ferdinand dining with astrologer Jeane Dixon,
January 1956.*

King Saud, left, of Saudi Arabia.

Queen Ingrid and King Frederik of Denmark.

(above) *Ethiopian Emperor Haile Selassie welcomes a guest to his reception at the hotel.* (left) *The elaborate buffet table stretching from the stage of the Grand Ballroom.*

King Hussein of Jordan is greeted at The Mayflower by the U.S. State Department's head of protocol, Alexis U. Johnson, March 25, 1959.

Their Imperial Highnesses, Prince and Princess Takamatsu of Japan, stayed at The Mayflower on their honeymoon trip in 1930 and were honored by an official reception with top government figures. It is said that the Prince shook hands with each of the over 2,000 guests.

The Shah of Iran, c. 1958.

President Bourguiba of Tunisia, arriving at The Mayflower for the reception given in his honor on May 5, 1961.

CHAPTER TWO

The Launching
of The Mayflower

$\mathcal{The}$ early 1920s were a time of great prosperity in Washington, and one of the most fashionable parts of town was the area along lower Connecticut Avenue. Once dismissed as a mud path in the middle of a farm called Port Royal, the avenue was now an elegant thoroughfare lined with embassies, expensive apartment houses, and a flourishing row of fine shops. It also had the distinction of being no more than a few minutes' walk from the White House, and only a few more from Capitol Hill.

What this fashionable area needed, decided Washington developer Allan E. Walker, was a stylish new hotel—preferably on the corner of Connecticut Avenue and De Sales Street, where he owned an acre and a half of choice property once occupied by the Convent of the Visitation.

To blueprint his dream, Walker turned to the New York architectural firm of Warren and Wetmore, then regarded as the premier designer of hotels in America. The firm's credits included New York's Ritz Carlton, Vanderbilt, Biltmore, Commodore, and Ambassador hotels, in addition to its major architectural coup—Grand Central Terminal. Warren and Wetmore worked with Washington architect Robert F. Beresford on the Mayflower's design.

Ground for the building was broken in July 1922. Unfortunately, Walker's site presented unanticipated problems. Beneath the surface, a troublesome stream forced the construction company to dig the foundation walls clear down to bedrock, thereby delaying building for months. Further complications came with the discovery of quicksand and several fossilized tree stumps—some more than eight feet across—estimated to be at least thirty thousand years old.

Because of these unforeseen delays, Walker ran out of money, and his dream turned into bitter disappointment. Just months before the hotel opened, Walker was forced to sell a controlling interest in the project to C. C. Mitchell, an officer in the American Bond and Mortgage company, one of Walker's major financial backers. Walker helplessly watched Mitchell and his partners erect what would have been called "The Walker Hotel", but was now "The Mayflower Hotel".

Connecticut Avenue traffic, c. 1928, in front of the Mayflower's main entrance. The hotel was designed by Warren and Wetmore, the same firm that designed Grand Central Station in New York City.

FORM AND FUNCTION

When The Mayflower unfurled its sails on February 18, 1925—three years after ground had been broken—no trace of the struggles remained. The majestic, cream-colored structure was finally finished. Ten stories high, it was made of steel, stone, concrete, brick, and marble. The cost, not including furnishings, was about one million dollars per story—an extravagant sum at the time. Today, a luxury hotel built in the same grand style would cost more than twelve million dollars per floor.

Warren and Wetmore's neoclassic design provided a brilliant solution to the problems posed by an irregularly shaped site. In the hands of lesser architects, the building might have been awkward, uncomfortable, or, at the very least, an inefficient use of precious urban land. Instead, the angular west face, with its two curved towers—combined with the imposing yet carefully proportioned north wing along De Sales Street—used the site to spectacular advantage.

The Mayflower's interior was designed to complement its exterior. Furnishings in the hotel cost over two million dollars. More than twenty-five thousand pieces of furniture were imported from New York to dress The Mayflower in style. It took two hundred freight cars to deliver this treasure to Washington. A crew worked day and night for three months just to put the furniture in place throughout the hotel.

One of the most talked-about features of the interior was the use of ornamentation, especially gold leaf and marble. At its opening, The Mayflower contained more gold leaf in its trimmings and decorations than any building in the country except for the Library of Congress. The marble, too, was impressive in its range, from pink Tennessee to St. Genevieve gold vein.

The hotel was conceived in three functional units: public rooms, rooms for transient guests, and an annex of apartments for more permanent visitors. No two guest rooms were outfitted alike, thereby avoiding the sameness that deprived so many other hotels of distinction. Every room had its own special charm. Individually chosen decorations included high-quality antique reproductions, silk draperies, and original watercolors, mezzotints, and etchings.

In the apartment Annex for permanent guests, the furnishings were even more lavish, designed to make the most sophisticated visitor feel at home. Suites were decorated with genuine antiques and an assortment of period furniture; the rooms contained Oriental rugs and window hangings made of satin damask and silk taffeta. Baths had silver-plated fixtures and glass-enclosed showers.

MUSEUM-QUALITY PUBLIC ROOMS

In addition to the main lobby, The Mayflower had a mezzanine, meeting rooms, restaurants, and private dining rooms, as well as a promenade gallery one-tenth of a mile long—the equivalent of two city blocks.

The lobby was palatial, in both feeling and size.

The original lobby as seen from the Connecticut Avenue entrance.

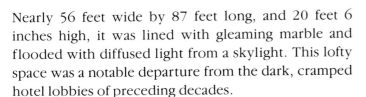

Nearly 56 feet wide by 87 feet long, and 20 feet 6 inches high, it was lined with gleaming marble and flooded with diffused light from a skylight. This lofty space was a notable departure from the dark, cramped hotel lobbies of preceding decades.

Surrounding the lobby on three sides was the mezzanine, reached by elevators and a stairway from below. It contained writing tables, lounges, and easy chairs for guests seeking a quiet and contemplative atmosphere.

Beyond the lobby one was drawn into the cool recesses of the large Palm Court. The room's green latticed, glass-domed ceiling; a splashing, shell-shaped fountain bathed in colored lights; and bird cages set among high palms—all suggested a tropical setting.

Opening from the Palm Court was the Presidential Dining Room, the main restaurant of the hotel. This room had a stately, patriotic feeling evoked by coats of arms from the various Commonwealths, portraits of the first four U.S. Presidents, and china and silverware bearing an image of the hotel's nautical namesake. Close by was the colonial style coffee shop, with an adjacent soda fountain.

Crossing the Palm Court, one entered the Promenade, extending from Connecticut Avenue to the entrance on 17th Street. The walls of this enormous gallery were lined with original works of art and antiques. They included seventeenth- and eighteenth-century French Aubusson tapestries; antique vases from Sèvres; period tables, chests, and consoles; fine porcelains; three paintings of the ship *Mayflower* by the American artist James G. Tyler; and life-size sculptures by M. Denys Puech, William Cooper, and Randolph Rogers. The grandest of these three marble

The richly decorated original Promenade.

An early photograph showing a seventeenth-century Aubusson tapestry on the wall of the Promenade. The tapestry is back in place today, following the hotel's restoration.

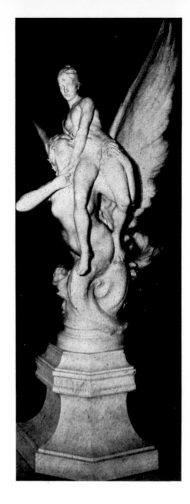

One of the original marble sculptures in the Mayflower lobby, "La Sirène", by Dennis Puech.

Today's Cafe Promenade was originally a tea room called the Palm Court. It featured daily dances, referred to as "tea dansants", under the direction of a Madame Mishtowt, the wife of a former naval attaché of the Russian Embassy. After the repeal of Prohibition, the Palm Court became The Mayflower Lounge, one of Washington's most popular meeting places.

sculptures was eight feet wide by six feet high. Entitled *La Seine*, it depicted a woman rising out of the sea with a boy on her shoulders. It was the work of Puech, a sculptor known for his monuments in Paris's Luxembourg Garden.

Not only was there much to see in the Promenade, but, with its lounges and easy chairs, it was also a comfortable and convenient place to meet with friends. The Promenade gave access to the Presidential Room, Palm Court, Grand Ballroom, Chinese Room, Annex lobby, and adjacent reception rooms, including the North Room and the East Room.

The Grand Ballroom, on the southern side of the ground floor, was one of the most spectacular halls in the country. Large enough for an auto show, it was painted in ivory, gold, and vermilion. It had a vaulted ceiling, black and gold marble pillars, lush gilt ornamentation, and murals painted by Venetian artist Ampelio Tonilio. Balcony boxes lined three sides. At the west end of the room was a disappearing stage, fully equipped for theatricals, musicales, and lectures, and a full-sized movie screen.

opening of the Radio Show, October 28, 1930, in the Grand Ballroom.

A 1930s view of The Promenade as seen from the 17th Street end, looking west to the main entrance.

Its location on the main floor was, according to architect Beresford, a deliberate break with convention. "It is a common experience in hotels where the ballroom is situated above the street floor to find a large ball or convention completely demoralizing the elevator service for guests", he wrote. "At The Mayflower . . . there is always freedom of access to it without disturbance to the other occupants of the hotel."

At the east end of the Ballroom was its foyer, called the Chinese Room. Often compared to Whistler's famous Peacock Room in the Freer Gallery, this room was decorated in the glowing reds and blues of Chinese-Chippendale style. The large oval dome decorated with Chinese figures was set off with gleaming lacquer, sumptuous hangings, and Oriental murals.

Beneath the Mayflower's main floor was the Garden, a handsome room with coppered ceilings, a large dance floor, a marble fountain, and landscape murals of Washington and Mount Vernon. The atmosphere suggested the outdoors, with warmly tinted high plaster walls and alcoves that looked like latticed arbors.

A HOTEL PLUS

The Mayflower had more than just surface beauty. In addition to the lavish architecture and décor, it pioneered in such amenities as a rudimentary air-cooling system, a central vacuum-cleaner system, and private bathrooms in all guest rooms, and in servants' quarters as well. The hotel had its own laundry, printing press, carpentry and upholstery repair shops, silver shop, emergency medical clinic with staff physician, and even a barbershop (for employees only). Guests had the convenience of a florist, stockbroker's office, and drugstore right on the premises—unprecedented in the 1920s.

When the Mayflower's apartment Annex opened, six months after the main building, the hotel provided its permanent residents with a separate commissary and catering department. Annex dwellers also had an entrance and lobby all to themselves so they could come and go in privacy, avoiding the bustle and crowds at the main entrance. The Annex lobby, on De Sales Street, had a round-the-clock attendant and receptionist.

In all, a thousand employees were required to run the hotel. Many of them came from abroad, where hotel service had a tradition of quality. Among the first hired was a Russian count who had lost his diplomatic post in France after the Communists took power in his native country.

FOOD, MARVELOUS FOOD . . .

The Mayflower was especially proud of its kitchens. The culinary equipment was the very latest. There was a staff of one hundred cooks, all European-trained. From the start, the kitchen prepared sixty-five hundred meals per day. The cuisine, which offered dishes of many nations, soon became famous in Washington.

There were separate cooking facilities for preparing

THE MAYFLOWER GOES "TALKIE"

The Grand Ballroom, set up for an assembly of 1500

Talking pictures being projected before a convention group

Sound motion pictures naturally followed the other appointments and details of modern equipment at The Mayflower...Here is one hotel specially planned for the correct accommodation of large or small meeting groups...There are more than 1000 beautifully furnished rooms, all with private bath and outside exposure...The Grand Ballroom and eight other public assembly rooms are located on the two lower floors...Incomparable cuisine, watchful service and old fashioned hospitality prevail . . .

When Television Becomes a Serviceable Reality for conventions, we will have it.

The MAYFLOWER

A full-page advertisement for The Mayflower, c. 1928. Talkies were very new, and there is even a mention of "television" as a future attraction of the hotel.

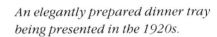

An elegantly prepared dinner tray being presented in the 1920s.

An early Mayflower barber, immaculate in his whites, awaits the next client.

each type of food, so there would be no undesirable mingling of scents and flavors. Every day the hotel's bakery turned out ten thousand rolls, three hundred loaves of French bread, and a hundred loaves of sandwich bread. The creamery produced fifty gallons of ice cream, and the soup kitchen filled a dozen stockpots, some holding as much as fifty gallons. In the preparation of meat dishes, separate kitchens were used for roasting, frying, broiling, and preparing cold cuts.

The chefs of The Mayflower traditionally tried to accommodate the ethnic palates and patriotic sensibilities of foreign guests. The kitchens strove to evoke the colors, if not the flavors, of their native lands. For instance, spun-sugar ribbons were used to indicate national colors on confections and table decorations, and the icing on cakes spelled out words of welcome

"Papa" Jarrin, left, founder of the Epicurean Club, talks shop with Chef Anthony Marcello in the hotel's kitchen, 1963.

Completely edible, the Mayflower's award-winning gingerbread house is viewed by some admirers, 1964.

in a dignitary's native tongue. Often some member of the staff was sent off to the Library of Congress to look up national emblems, flags, mottoes, or the like.

One example of research paying off was a buffet reception in October 1954 given by Liberian Ambassador and Mrs. Clarence Simpson for Liberian President William V. S. Tubman and a thousand guests. One of the striking features of the fifty-five-foot buffet, which, according to Ruth Dean of the *Evening Star,* "looked like something out of the Arabian nights", was a bas-relief tableau. The tableau, a scene of Liberia, was complete with a waterfall and a stream in which live goldfish frisked about. This marvel, made of ice, was just another afternoon's work for the presiding chef. Also gracing the table was a special flower arrangement—red roses, white chrysanthemums, and blue delphiniums—in the colors of both the Liberian and American flags.

One of the best-remembered feats of the Mayflower kitchen was the baking and assembling of a completely edible fantasy. In 1964 an eighty pound gingerbread house won the "Artistic Individual Masterpiece Award" at the Fifth Salon of Culinary Arts, cosponsored by the Epicurean Club of Washington and the Washington Restaurant Association. Three feet high, it was made of honey, flour, spices, and thirty pounds of sugar. The interior was plastered with five pounds of chocolate, the sloping roof featured five hundred mint shingles, and its snow-colored (white frosting) lawn was fenced with more than three hundred gingerbread logs. There were marzipan figures of Hansel and Gretel, the witch, and St. Nicholas. Also depicted in edibles were a sleigh, a water well, trees, walkways, and chimney smoke.

"Hansel and Gretel have finally solved their housing problem", said Elinn Lee in the *Washington Post.* "The fairy tale characters have found an elegant town house that makes their old candy house in the woods look like a shack . . . the Hansel and Gretel holiday house is truly a culinary creation."

After being on display in the Promenade for two weeks, the prize-winning gingerbread house found some wide-eyed caretakers: It was given to the children at St. Ann's Infant Home.

Over the years, the Mayflower's culinary flair received many good reviews. Perhaps the most eloquent and charming was from newspaper society editor Sam Haldenstein in 1948, following the thirty-seventh annual convention of the American Hotel Association in the Mayflower's Grand Ballroom:

Of myriad number, I daresay, have been the buffets I have attended from the days of the old Waldorf Astoria to this Sunday night in manager Neal Mack's Mayflower Hotel. Never have I seen, nor partaken of, so varied, so beautifully set forth and arranged, so temptingly delicious, so exquisitely fashioned a buffet, in all the forms and all the dishes, and so marvelously decorated with countless candelabra and contrasting and blending flower arrangements. Never have I seen before a table the equal of catering manager Fred Wiesinger's that auspicious night. . . .

The question was where to begin and what to take. But we did begin and we did take; the pâté de foie gras; the cold succulent salmon; the broiled lobsters; the ducklings en gelée; the squab chickens; the turkeys; the whole tongues in aspic, glazed, so expertly carved; the prime ribs of beef, cold, sliced and served with calf's-foot jelly; the salads; the whole tomatoes stuffed with crabmeat. Please, please believe me I did not choose them all; I had the will to; but not the daring.

A wide variety of cold buffet dishes, including shellfish, cheese, pastry, and fruit. This elaborate presentation reflects the hotel's tradition of culinary flair.

SCENIC VIEW FOR THE WORLD'S WHO'S WHO

When completed, The Mayflower had 1,059 rooms, making it one of the largest hotels in America. Transient guests occupied 650 rooms; the remainder, in the Annex, were grouped into 112 apartments, ranging in size from one to nine rooms. Each offered a fine view of Washington. Some windows looked out on fashionable Connecticut Avenue. From others, guests could see the White House, the Washington Monument, or the Capitol.

The Presidential and Vice Presidential suites were the most luxurious. Designed to emulate the royal chambers of European grand hotels, they occupied two entire floors of the Annex. Each suite had twelve rooms, with five bedrooms (each with private bath and glass-enclosed shower), a foyer, drawing room or salon, library, dining room, secretary's room, kitchen, and maid's room. These suites, and most apartments, also contained working fireplaces to create a homey atmosphere, and a complete service of china, linen, and silver.

In the 1920s the Mayflower's room rates were re-markably low. At a time when a full set of car tires cost $90 and a custom-made suit went for $75, single rooms began at $5 a night, double rooms at $7, and suites with parlor and bedroom at $18. This means that a luxury double room cost about one-tenth the price of a fine suit in 1925, while today the equivalent room would be more like one-half the price of a suit—a clear indication that hotel charges have risen at a much faster rate than other commodities. (A Mayflower ad in the early 1930s, in the depth of the Depression, gives the prices as $4 single and $6 double.)

The first person to sign the Mayflower's guest register, on February 19, 1925, was Major H. R. Lemly, a retired U.S. soldier and scholar. Soon, however, the register read like an American *Who's Who,* brimming with Vanderbilts, Mellons, Firestones, Fords, members of Washington high society, affluent northerners en route to Florida for the winter, executives on business trips, and many of the national and international elite in politics, the professions, and the arts.

The Annex got off to a famous start with the arrival

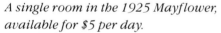

Two of the hotel's original suites, each about $18 per day.

A single room in the 1925 Mayflower, available for $5 per day.

Veteran doorman Bob Beaver assisting an arriving guest.

The original sign outside the Mayflower's Annex apartments.

tury French actress Sarah Bernhardt. The Curtis suite quickly became the official gathering place of the Hoover Administration. Curtis, a bachelor, relied on his sister Dolly Gann to act as hostess.

By 1932, there were twenty-three members of Congress living at The Mayflower, among them Senator Huey P. Long, Jr., of Louisiana. Many more senators resided in the Annex over the decades—Speaker of the House William B. Bankhead and his family (including daughter Tallulah), A. B. "Happy" Chandler of Kentucky, John W. Bricker of Ohio, George Malone of Nevada, Charles L. McNary of Oregon, John J. William of Delaware, Arthur Cuppler of Kansas, Carter Glass of Virginia, Walter George of Georgia, Everett M. Dirksen of Illinois, Edward M. Kennedy of Massachusetts, and Edmund S. Muskie of Maine. Other government notables included Supreme Court Justices Stanley F. Reed and Benjamin N. Cardozo, Secretary of the Interior Harold L. Ickes, diplomat and cabinet officer Patrick J. Hurley, Postmaster General and Democratic National Committee Chairman James A. Farley, and Republican National Committee Chairman Harrison E. Spangler.

A famous Annex occupant was Milton Kronheim, a prominent Washington businessman, who stayed for more than thirty years—one of the longest stays of any Mayflower guest. It was not uncommon, however, for Annex guests to remain for a decade or more.

of Herbert Hoover's Vice-President, Charles Curtis, who lived and entertained at The Mayflower throughout his four-year term. His suite occupied an entire floor of the Annex. It featured five bedrooms and a library decorated with Oriental rugs and period pieces, including a Louis XVI cabinet with painted panels that was said to have belonged to the great nineteenth-cen-

Sitting room of a Mayflower suite, c. 1940.

(left) *Mrs. Edward Everett (Dolly) Gann, sister of Herbert Hoover's Vice-President, Charles Curtis, c. 1930.*

(right) *Vice-President (1929-33) Charles Curtis, followed by Mr. and Mrs. Gann, and escorted by then Major George Patton, later to become the famed World War II general, arrive at the Polo Ball at The Mayflower, 1931. The arch of polo sticks was made by the season's debutantes.*

Senator and Mrs. John Bankhead and Speaker of the House (seated) and Mrs. William Bankhead (parents of Tallulah) listening to the radio in the early 1930s in the latters' Annex apartment.

Milton Kronheim, prominent Washington businessman, who lived at The Mayflower for more than thirty years.

Fashionable Folk

Three fashion sketches by artist Julia Boyd from a Mayflower publication in 1928. The original captions identify the models as important socialites and describe each outfit in the high-fashion language of the day.

The Mayflower's annual New Year's Eve party in the State Room. For 1986, the theme was the 1920s.

Annual New Year's Eve party given by the Consort Club, Washington's elite black society. The prestigious ball has been held at the Mayflower since 1969. At right, former mayor Walter Washington and wife Bennetta.

SPECIAL WOMEN AT THE MAYFLOWER

Certain political wives left their marks on the hotel through the years. The earliest was Evelyn (Evie) Robert, wife of Lawrence Wood Robert, Secretary of the Democratic National Committee and Assistant Secretary of the Treasury from 1933 to 1936.

Evie, daughter of the original, stymied Mayflower builder, Allan E. Walker, lived at the hotel for more than forty years until her death in 1972. She was once voted "Miss Mayflower" by the hotel staff for her largesse. In characteristic fashion, she would bring truckloads of Christmas trees from her Virginia farm for distribution to all the employees.

She was noted for her originality and disregard for convention. A great lover of animals, she not only worked for the city's zoo but also occasionally kept lion cubs in her apartment and walked through the lobby with an alligator on a leash.

Geraldine Smith of the *Philadelphia Inquirer* noted Evie's nonconformist tendencies, recalling one impromptu afternoon cocktail party in the Roberts' Annex suite: "The motley collection of guests included a portrait painter, who was preserving Evie for posterity; the cop on the beat; an Army major who did card tricks and sang opera; a character who arrived carrying a broom; Evie's lawyer; and a violinist and guitar player, summoned from the Mayflower bar." Reporter Smith was further astonished to see Evie vanish into her boudoir at 6:30 P.M., reappearing in an evening gown to attend a dinner with the Cuban Ambassador. As she strode from the room, she said, "Last one out lock the door".

Perhaps the most important woman associated with The Mayflower was Eleanor Roosevelt, niece of Theodore Roosevelt and a distant cousin of her husband, Franklin. Her hard work for a variety of social causes marked her as much more than just the wife of a President.

During FDR's twelve years in office, she carried out much of her work at functions held at The Mayflower. It was at a luncheon there in 1933 that she accepted the leadership of the National Women's Committee for Human Needs. In her acceptance speech, she expressed her belief that support of community welfare services throughout the country was essential to help the nation recover from the Depression. The following year, between formal charity balls and social affairs, such as the Junior League Ball, she spoke at numerous community and association meetings, always expressing her humanitarian concerns. Addressing the Association of Private School Teachers, for instance, she urged the educators to do their utmost to develop more initiative and imagination in the minds of their pupils. Speaking before the General Federation of Women's Clubs, she suggested that they turn their attention to the problems of unemployed women.

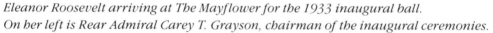

Eleanor Roosevelt arriving at The Mayflower for the 1933 inaugural ball.
On her left is Rear Admiral Carey T. Grayson, chairman of the inaugural ceremonies.

Mrs. Franklin D. Roosevelt is shown here at a 1946 meeting of the Women's National Press Club held in the East Room. In the front row, from left to right, are May Craig, Bess Furman Armstrong (president of the club), Mrs. Roosevelt, and Isabelle Griffin.

Eleanor Roosevelt knew how to relax at The Mayflower, too. Along with other Presidents' wives and widows, such as Edith Wilson and Helen Taft, she often attended the famous morning musicales in the Grand Ballroom.

Mrs. Roosevelt chats with Mary Dawson at a Jackson Day dinner, 1938.

Alice Roosevelt Longworth, daughter of Theodore Roosevelt, signing the guest book in the Presidential Dining Room.

The main dining room of the Nicholas Restaurant.

One of the private dining rooms of the Nicholas.

President Truman with wife Bess and daughter Margaret at a Mayflower function.

Margaret Truman and Missouri Senator Stuart Symington amused by the Republican symbol during a 1954 banquet.

In 1954, nine hundred Republican women helped Mamie Eisenhower celebrate her fifty-eighth birthday at a luncheon at The Mayflower. All nine cabinet wives were on hand for the occasion, each bearing a gift for the First Lady—from an oversized magenta sun hat to an antique Sheffield candelabrum. There was also a surprise appearance by television comedian Red Skelton.

Red Skelton at Mamie Eisenhower's 1954 birthday party. The comedian quipped: "I like coming to a party like this. I get to entertain. If it was her husband's party, I would have to caddy."

The women dined on breast of capon under glass, asparagus tips polonaise, and potatoes au gratin. Next, a long procession of waiters marched into the room, each carrying a baked Alaska. Mrs. Eisenhower was then presented with a large, three-tiered, white-frosted birthday cake with one candle on top. After she made a wish, the lights were dimmed, and each guest was asked to light a candle. The women rose, sang ''Happy Birthday'' in unison, then blew out all nine hundred candles at once.

Next came Skelton, who burst out of a seven-foot-high ''birthday box'' behind the head table. ''Everyone else had a baked Alaska, and she gets a baked ham'', he quipped. ''I like coming to a party like this'', he added. ''I get to entertain. If it was her husband's party, I would have to caddy.''

Mamie Eisenhower at her 1953 birthday party given by the Women's National Press Club. Alongside her is Polly Bergen.

*Jacqueline Kennedy being greeted by the Mayflower's ban-
quet manager, Walter Seligman, c. 1962. At right is Roger
Stevens, the first Director of the Kennedy Center for the
Performing Arts.*

*Lady Bird Johnson at the President's inaugural,
1965.*

Mrs. Richard Nixon greets friends at a Saints and Sinners Club party in 1953.

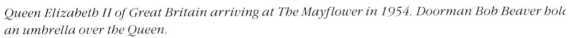

Queen Elizabeth II of Great Britain arriving at The Mayflower in 1954. Doorman Bob Beaver holds an umbrella over the Queen.

THE MAYFLOWER'S EARLY DAYS

Before opening its doors to the public, the hotel had its own coming-out party—thrown with the elegance and style that were to become its hallmark for future generations.

On February 17, 1925, the eve of the grand opening, seven hundred fifty special guests were given a taste of what the rest of Washington would experience the next day. Those who had designed, constructed, and equipped the hotel were invited to celebrate at a gala party for themselves. Dozens of well-known people from the political, social, and financial worlds also attended, among them Secretary of Labor James J. Davis, the principal speaker on that occasion, who declared that the hotel was "a symbol of individual initiative".

The next morning the *Washington Star* described The Mayflower as "one of the most magnificent [hotels] in the country". That night, fifteen hundred people thronged to the official opening festivities. They held invitations that had been mailed with Pilgrim tercentenary one-cent U.S. postage stamps, reissued specially for the opening of the hotel. Those first May-flower guests nibbled extravagant delicacies in the Presidential Dining Room and danced to Vincent Lopez's orchestra. As they left, they were given as souvenirs Pilgrim half-dollars, which had been issued in 1920 to commemorate the three hundredth anniversary of the landing of the ship *Mayflower* at Plymouth Rock. Again the *Washington Star* commented on the affair, calling it the "very last word in hotel service".

Of course, not everything works out perfectly when a newly launched hotel hoists its sails. Shortly after the opening, The Mayflower booked its first large convention—a meeting organized by the International Parliamentary Union, attended mainly by delegates from foreign countries. As was the custom in hotels abroad, particularly in Europe, the IPU guests put their shoes out in the hall at night, to be shined and returned by morning. Unfortunately, the Mayflower staff was unaware of this exotic practice. Baffled by the shoes sitting out in the corridors, the bellboys and valets collected them and dropped them willy-nilly into laundry bags.

Two 1930s ads invite guests to "Visit the Presidential Dining Room, one of the truly famous restaurants of the world, or the Coffee Shop which features a most reasonably priced table d'hôte menu".

The Mayflower

Connecticut Avenue, midway between The White House & Dupont Circle.

Washington, D.C.

Permanent home
of Statesmen
Diplomats
and Society

Lobbies and Public
rooms artificially
cooled
in summer

VISITORS to the Nation's Capital after the middle of February, will enjoy the maximum of comfort at The Mayflower, Washington's newest and finest hotel. ~ ~ ~ Advance reservations now being accepted.

HERE you will find rich beauty and intimate refinements to please the most discriminating patron. ~ A real welcome awaits you, and no effort will be spared to make you feel at home.

Telephone
Main 9800

Cable Address
Mayflower

CONNECTICUT AVENUE

De Sales and Seventeenth Streets, Northwest.

The first Mayflower advertisement, 1925, emphasizing the hotel's deluxe atmosphere and aspirations.

Next morning, the delegates opened their doors to find their shoes not only not shined but missing. When the hotel's manager became aware of the mistake, he prayed that the earth would open up and swallow him. This didn't happen, so he was obliged to advise his guests that their shoes could be retrieved in the Grand Ballroom, where they had been laid out—unshined and, worse yet, unpaired. What ensued was an unforgettable scene—scores of bewildered and irate foreigners making their way in stockinged feet to the Ballroom, there to shuffle around trying to match one black shoe with another!

Such gaffes, however funny, were fortunately rare at The Mayflower. Indeed, it tended toward the opposite extreme. For instance, in preparing for that same international convention, the hotel made a logistical coup in anticipating the mass arrival of its guests. Knowing that there would be sixteen hundred luggage pieces coming from New York to Washington all at once, three Mayflower baggage clerks were dispatched to New York to arrange for a train earlier than that of the guests to transport the luggage to Washington. En route, the clerks methodically tagged each of the bags with its intended room number. By the time the delegates checked in, all sixteen hundred pieces were waiting for them in their rooms.

Dedication of the Mayflower's Pan American Room on February 23, 1929. Left to right are Daniel J. O'Brien, general manager; Dr. Leo S. Rowe, Director General of the Pan American Union; Dr. Orestes Ferrara, Cuban Ambassador to the United States; Mr. S. Giurgel do Amaral, Ambassador of Brazil; and the Honorable Francis White, Assistant Secretary of State.

The Mayflower's opening day, February 18, 1925, with the staff awaiting the hotel's first arrivals in the reception area. Fifteen hundred guests were present for the opening festivities.

Dignitaries arriving at The Mayflower.

PRESIDENTIAL INAUGURALS

The event that established The Mayflower as a leader among Washington hotels occurred about two weeks after the grand opening. It was President Calvin Coolidge's charity inaugural ball, which took place on March 4, 1925, in the Grand Ballroom.* The country was in the mood to celebrate, but the President was not. He was at that moment mourning his sixteen-year-old son's untimely death from blood poisoning. Choosing not to attend the ball, Coolidge sent Vice-President Charles Dawes in his place.

The President's absence did not put a damper on the festivities, however. The four thousand invited guests swelled to six thousand zealous revelers, eventually spilling over into all the Mayflower's function rooms. Guests included nineteen state governors and the new French ambassador, Émile Daeschner, who made his first American public appearance at this ball.

Early that afternoon the doors of The Mayflower were closed to the general public. At 8:30 in the evening elegant women began arriving, in their satin crepe and chiffon gowns, on the arms of Washington's top social, official, and diplomatic figures (top figures

*Inauguration day was March 4 until 1937, when it was changed to January 20.

in those days were almost always men).

At 10:00 P.M., drums and a fanfare announced the guests of honor—the state governors, U.S. senators and representatives, and members of the cabinet. The last to arrive was Vice-President Dawes, dressed in full military regalia, and then the ball officially began. Music sounded through the night, played by military dance bands, Roger Kahn's Hotel Biltmore Orchestra from New York, and Vincent Lopez's orchestra. The ballroom floor was too crowded for dancing, but most guests didn't mind—they had come to see and be seen. A great social success, the ball also succeeded in raising $40,000 for charity—a sum equivalent to about $2 million in 1987.

The Coolidge inaugural was the first of many such celebrations to be held at The Mayflower, but for those who remembered the party, no other inaugural ball quite matched that first affair. Part of its glamour came from the excitement of being in Washington in the giddily prosperous decade after World War I; but an equally significant part was taking in the freshness and beauty of the new hotel itself. With the Coolidge inaugural ball, The Mayflower opened its doors to history—and they have remained open ever since.

President Harry S. Truman had no inaugural ball when he succeeded to the office on the death of Franklin Delano Roosevelt. He is shown here being honored at the traditional Jackson Day Dinner on March 23, 1946, with his daughter Margaret. At right is Mrs. Fred Vinson, wife of the Chief Justice of the U.S. Supreme Court.

(opposite) *The Calvin Coolidge inaugural ball, March 4, 1925, the first official political event at The Mayflower.*

The John F. Kennedy inaugural ball, January 1961, with Mrs. Kennedy in a white chiffon sheath. Vice-President Lyndon Johnson is on the left. To the right, in a white fur stole, is Lady Bird Johnson.

President Carter, January 1977, stands for his welcome in the Grand Ballroom, along with daughter Amy and wife Rosalynn.

President Ronald Reagan addresses the celebrants at his 1981 inaugural ball.

Press coverage of Johnson-Humphrey
headquarters in the Grand Ballroom.

A Mayflower bellman adjusting the rigging of a model of the hotel's namesake, which was displayed in the lobby when the hotel first opened.

Throughout the more than sixty years of its existence, The Mayflower has proclaimed a historical and nautical motif. Named for the ship that carried the Pilgrims from Europe to New England, the hotel itself was opened shortly after the three hundredth anniversary of the historic landing at Plymouth Rock—hence the commemorative coins and stamps given to its first guests.

The Mayflower *ship theme has always been highly visible. There is a large model of the vessel on display in the lobby, as well as three* Mayflower *paintings by James G. Tyler. One depicts the* Mayflower *sailing into the sunset;* another shows the Pilgrims being rowed ashore in boats from the mother ship; and the third portrays John Alden, Priscilla Mullens, John Carver, William Brewster, and Miles Standish in the foreground, with the Mayflower at anchor offshore.

The ship appears also in the crest used on the chinaware and on the elevator doors. And the historical-nautical theme found its way, of course, into the names of the hotel's house publications: The Rudder, Pilgrim's Progress, *and* The Mayflower's Log.

Anniversary Number
Vol. IV   March, 1928   No. 1

Covers of The Mayflower's Log *from 1928 to 1939 showing the varied graphic styles of the time.* The Log *was sold for twenty-five cents a copy.*

Edicion Latino Americana—Enero 1930

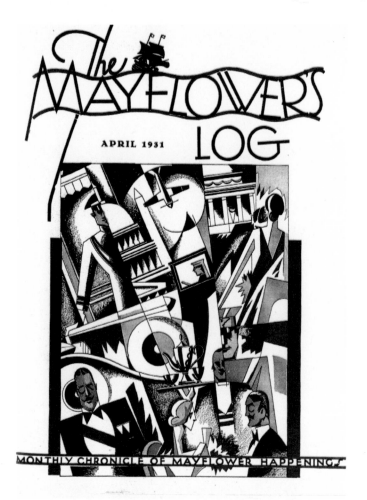

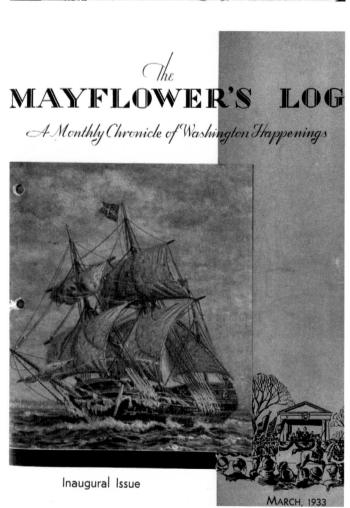

*Committee meeting held in the State Room to select the site
of the 1988 Democratic Party presidential nominating
convention. An announcement is being made to the press
by Committee Chairman Nathan Landow that Atlanta,
Georgia, was chosen.*

OFFICERS OF THE MAYFLOWER

MR. R. L. POLLIO,
Manager

●

MR. C. J. MACK,
Chief Accountant

MR. OSGOOD ROBERTS,
Director of Publicity

MRS. WM. LAIRD DUNLOP, JR.,
Director of Social Bureau

MR. J. F. SCHLOTTERBECK,
Front Office Manager

MR. A. B. VAN VOORHEES,
Front Office Manager

MR. GEORGE F. RALSTON, JR.,
*Assistant Manager
in Charge of Conventions*

MR. E. R. HAMMER,
*Assistant Manager
in Charge of Apartments*

MR. E. A. ELDRED,
Credit Manager

MR. LEO H. GRAVES,
Night Manager

MR. FRED WIESINGER,
Maitre d'hotel

MR. NICHOLAS MARCHITELLI,
Chef de Cuisine

MR. ALFRED PAZOSKA,
Banquet Manager

MR. THOMAS J. SHANLEY,
Steward

MR. GEORGE L. DENNIS,
Superintendent, Room Service

MISS RUBY SIMS
Coffee Shop Manager

MR. ANDREW KIRSCHNER,
Head Waiter, Dining Room

MR. W. H. DUPAR,
Chief Engineer

MISS JANET MCCALLUM,
Housekeeper

MR. W. J. MULLEN,
*Superintendent
of Uniformed Service*

MR. J. R. SIMPSON,
Chief House Officer

●

DR. F. A. HORNADAY,
House Physician

SEPTEMBER, 1932

●CONTENTS

Dr. Erich Salomon

Front Desk

THE MAYFLOWER'S LOG

The MAYFLOWER'S LOG is published on the first of each month by The MAYFLOWER Hotel for the information and entertainment of its guests. Offices are located on the Mezzanine Floor. Mr. Osgood Roberts, Editor. Copyright, 1932.

Contents pages from 1932 and 1933 editions of The Mayflower's Log.

OFFICERS OF THE MAYFLOWER

MR. R. L. POLLIO,
Manager

●

MR. C. J. MACK,
Chief Accountant

MR. OSGOOD ROBERTS,
Director of Publicity

MRS. WM. LAIRD DUNLOP, JR.,
Director of Social Bureau

MR. E. R. HAMMER,
Assistant Manager

MR. TRAVERS J. CROCKER
Assistant Manager

MR. A. B. VAN VOORHEES,
Front Office Manager

MR. J. F. SCHLOTTERBECK,
*Assistant Manager and
Special Business Representative*

MR. E. A. ELDRED,
Credit Manager

MR. LEO H. GRAVES,
Night Manager

MR. FRED WIESINGER,
Maitre d'hotel

MR. NICHOLAS MARCHITELLI,
Chef de Cuisine

MR. ALFRED PAZOSKA,
Banquet Manager

MR. THOMAS J. SHANLEY,
Steward

MR. GEORGE L. DENNIS,
Superintendent, Room Service

MISS RUBY SIMS
Coffee Shop Manager

MR. ANDREW KIRSCHNER,
Head Waiter, Dining Room

MRS. B. H. KNIGHT,
*Superintendent, Telephone
Service*

MR. W. H. DUPAR,
Chief Engineer

MISS JANET MCCALLUM,
Housekeeper

MR. W. J. MULLEN,
*Superintendent
of Uniformed Service*

MR. J. R. SIMPSON,
Chief House Officer

●

DR. F. A. HORNADAY,
House Physician

MARCH, 1933

●CONTENTS

Horydczak

THE MAYFLOWER'S LOG

The MAYFLOWER'S LOG is published on the first of each month by The MAYFLOWER Hotel for the information and entertainment of its guests. Offices are located on the Mezzanine Floor. Mr. Osgood Roberts, Editor. Copyright, 1933. Price, 25 cents per copy, $2.50 per year.

Wedding ceremony in the Grand Ballroom.

A wedding reception in the East Room.

A Mayflower buffet setting.

CHAPTER THREE

Black Tie, Front Door; No Tie, Back Door — The Depression Years

The Great Depression that began with the stock market crash in 1929 created some dramatic contrasts at The Mayflower. The balls and galas continued in the grand old style (albeit with less frequency), but at the same time the hotel's owners were determined to respond to the reality of the times and to the wants of the needy.

A PARTY IN QUESTIONABLE TASTE

The excesses of those whose wealth was unaffected by the Depression, viewed against the squalid poverty of the 1930s, tended to underscore and even mock the plight of the nation as a whole. Unforgettable—perhaps unforgivable—was the debutante ball thrown by oil tycoon Henry L. Doherty for his daughter Helen Lee Eames Doherty on the day after Christmas, 1930. It was an affair that still ranks as one of the most extravagant in the history of the capital, with fifteen hundred black-tie guests, including Vice-President Charles Curtis, and star entertainment imported from New York. At the same time that limousines were pulling up at the front of the hotel, however, scores of hungry, unemployed Washingtonians were lining up at a nearby garage for a bowl of soup at the Mayflower's emergency canteen, organized by the hotel's management.

Weeks before the party took place, the press reported that young Helen Doherty had purchased a dozen sports cars to give to chosen guests, such as King Alfonso XIII of Spain, whom she had met while studying at the University of Madrid. As the publicity grew, so did the avalanche of angry letters to the Doherty family. The car-giving was called off—at least until after the debut—and was replaced by a less ostentatious gift plan. A centerpiece with a religious

Miss Helen Lee Eames Doherty as she appeared in a Mayflower publication, 1930. The original caption states that she "was presented to society at the most brilliant ball of the season . . ." In fact, the Depression era party was infamous for its ostentation in a time of desperate poverty.

The Cafe Promenade Sunday buffet brunch with music.

One of the restored 1920s murals by Edward Laning in the Cafe Promenade.

Christmas scene was prepared for the head table. Ribbons attached to a miniature church in the scene fanned out to the guests' place cards. Alongside these cards were the party favors: sterling silver cigarette lighters for the gentlemen and 18-karat-gold vanity boxes for the ladies.

To keep out crashers, a corps of social secretaries stood on guard, along with "ropes, flunkeys, card takers, guest lists, a copy of the new Social Register and the Army Official list", reported *Washington Daily News* columnist George Abell. "Among the guests who passed inspection were the reigning king and queen of Washington's social set, Vice President Charles Curtis and his sister Dolly Gann. . . . [the guests] represented nine nationalities and a wide jumble of ranks and grades", Abell continued. "One saw on every side the most startling contrasts. There were military cadets, Annapolis plebes, debutantes, dowagers, hotel clerks, New York financiers, White House aides, black-tied college youths, ambassadors, Army officers, Cabinet ladies, Senators—an endless variety. There were Spaniards, South Africans, Poles, Chileans, Ecuadoreans, Albanians, Swiss, Egyptians, and Turks."

Ignoring the hardships faced by so many people during that heart-wrenching Christmas season, everything at the party was provided in painfully conspicuous abundance. Massed poinsettias, banked with southern smilax and evergreens, were everywhere in evidence. The Chinese Room, where the Dohertys stood to receive their guests, was transformed into a flower garden with cavernous baskets of roses of practically every known variety and color. Orchid corsages were so plentiful that Miss Doherty made ropes out of them and flung them around people's necks.

The entire first floor of the hotel was given over to the party—the Chinese Room, the Grand Ballroom,

Debutantes in 1930 who were among the riding group attending the "Hunting Pink" Ball at the hotel.

the Palm Court, and the Presidential Dining Room. Singer Jessica Dragonette, then at the height of her popularity, was part of the attraction. While hundreds crowded around her in the Grand Ballroom, hundreds of thousands more heard her on the air. In an extraordinary, unprecedented move, the Dohertys had arranged for the party to be aired live on coast-to-coast radio.

Tradition of the Debutante Ball

Although the Doherty affair was by far the most flamboyant coming-out party held at The Mayflower, it was by no means the last one. Washington society continued to present its young women at Mayflower parties large and small. Debutantes made their social bows in the Grand Ballroom in settings as diverse as Vienna and Hawaii and in a wide variety of period costumes. Almost thirty years after the notorious Doherty debut, Charlotte Kidder made social headlines with her coming-out party for nearly a thousand guests. For the event, designer Valerian Rybor

turned the Mayflower's Grand Ballroom into a facsimile of the Paris Opera, and the gold decorations in the ballroom were regilded.

Until the beginning of World War II, coming-out parties were very expensive affairs arranged for individual debutantes by their families. In 1941, the mothers of eight of the season's debs decided to cut their costs by having a joint debut. This was the first of the famous Washington Debutante Balls. The highlight of the social season, these balls were conceived as an economy measure, but soon became status

ARTS AND THE MAYFLOWER

Almost from the beginning, The Mayflower had a stream of visiting artists, writers, and performers actively contributing to the hotel's ambiance. In 1930, while an exhibition of thirty sculptures and paintings by Auguste Rodin was in the hotel, there was a simultaneous show of the Swiss sculptor Ernst Durig, once one of Rodin's students. Durig stayed at the hotel during this period. Art exhibits in the public rooms continued through the years, featuring works by nationally and internationally known artists. During World War II, Helena Rubenstein loaned her art collection, including several Picassos, to the hotel for an exhibition to help raise money for war relief.

Music was another important part of the Mayflower's tradition. Starting in the late 1920s, society hostess Mrs. Lawrence Townsend organized morning musicales in the Grand Ballroom for hotel guests and select Washingtonians. These were virtuoso concert recitals, characterized by formality and decorum.

"The invitation is such an attractive one that you simply cannot decline it", recollected Frances Parkinson Keyes, writer, socialite, and senator's wife, "but you had to allow a little more time for your toilet—feeling thankful that you had a Lucrenze frock and a Camille Roger hat to wear, for everyone goes and everyone wears her best bib and tucker".

What made these musicales so popular for so long was the talent of Townsend, a composer in her own right, who courageously featured both musical newcomers and internationally known musicians. It was at a Townsend musicale, for example, that French pianist and composer Robert Casadesus made his Washington debut.

Among other performers who graced The Mayflower were pianists Arthur Rubinstein, Rudolph Serkin, Egon Petri, Ernest Schelling, and Emile Baume; violinists Jacques Thibaut and Paul Kuchanskie; sopranos Kirsten Flagstad, Lotte Lehmann, Rosa Ponselle, Maria Muller, and Grace Moore; baritone Lawrence Tibbett; and tenors Richard Crooks, Lauritz Melchior, and Rudolph Laubenthal.

Eleanor Roosevelt, 1940, attending the exhibition of Helena Rubinstein's modern art collection in The Mayflower. According to The Mayflower's Log, *the First Lady stopped "to study Picasso's much discussed impressionistic rendering titled 'Inspiration'".*

symbols for the capital's debutantes and their families.

If the Washington Debutante Balls were less costly for each family, they were no less elaborate than in the past. Typical was the 1964 Ball, when eighty-five daughters of Washington society made their bows in an elaborate Victorian garden setting. At one end of the Ballroom was a Victorian bandstand; at the other end was a pink-and-white

summer house, from which each deb emerged on the arm of her father. The debutantes, dressed in long white Victorian gowns, carried pink carnations that echoed the décor.

Some families still prefer to arrange individual debuts for their daughters, but the Mayflower's Washington Debutante Ball continues to be the capital's most prestigious annual social event.

The musicales were prestigious, inspirational events. "In the ballroom, you suddenly feel transplanted into the Middle Ages", Mrs. Keyes reminisced.

For the walls of cream, crimson, and gold and the hangings of azure and silver are strangely suggestive of the pennants and tapestries and arras of those great and gorgeous bygone days of knights in armor. You almost expect to see a herald, gay in tinsel trappings, advance and lift a gilded trumpet to his scarlet lips, instead of a plump, personable little man in a

strange combination of formal morning and informal sports costume who is bowing to a scattering applause. An instant later the exquisite liquid melody of Chopin follows and "Change d'Espagne" carries you off to Seville and Granada.

Over the years, audiences included leading members of Washington's diplomatic and social sets, including wives of presidents, congressmen, cabinet members, and Supreme Court justices. Of males there were only a scattered few.

Spanish-born pianist José Iturbi, who appeared in a number of Hollywood movies, entertains at one of Mrs. Townsend's musicales, c. 1943.

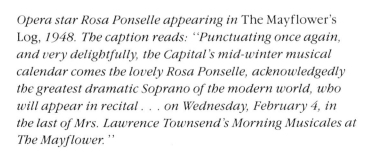

Opera star Rosa Ponselle appearing in The Mayflower's Log, *1948. The caption reads: "Punctuating once again, and very delightfully, the Capital's mid-winter musical calendar comes the lovely Rosa Ponselle, acknowledgedly the greatest dramatic Soprano of the modern world, who will appear in recital . . . on Wednesday, February 4, in the last of Mrs. Lawrence Townsend's Morning Musicales at The Mayflower."*

"All too soon it seems the concert is over", sighed Mrs. Keyes, "and you are gathering your furs around you and looking for your luncheon hostess—for everyone stays to lunch after the musicale. Mondell, whose husband served as representative of Wyoming for many years with great distinction, has been kind enough to include you among her guests. And soon you are chatting gaily over fruit cocktail and chicken à la king."

For more than two decades Townsend's musical mornings brought superb performances to Washing-ton's music lovers. At her hundredth musicale, on January 10, 1938, she received pink roses from the White House; a special tribute from conductor Arturo Toscanini; a telegram of admiring compatriotism from Albert Morris Bagby, host of the famous morning musicales in New York's Astor Hotel; and one hundred American beauty roses from the Mayflower management. Following World War II and the subsequent Hilton takeover of The Mayflower, the era of the Townsend musicales came to an end on February 4, 1948.

FEEDING THE HUNGRY

Even in the nation's capital, where the federal bureaucracy shielded residents from the full force of the Depression, unemployment had become an awesome problem; each day there were swelling numbers of people looking for work or handouts.

Daniel O'Brien, the Mayflower's first president and general manager (1925–32), was deeply concerned about the distress of the unemployed. He asked the Salvation Army how he could help, and was told that what the city urgently needed was a place where hungry job-seekers could find a wholesome meal at noon—the hour when their spirits were usually at their lowest.

O'Brien arranged for the owners of a vacant garage near The Mayflower to make it available as an emergency canteen. As word of the project spread, local merchants as well as the hotel donated food. O'Brien not only volunteered the hotel's staff and resources, but also carefully designed the canteen so that it would not have the grim atmosphere of a down-and-out soup kitchen.

Seated at long, clean tables, the hungry were given hot lunches six days a week. They were served by the hotel's management staff, members of service organizations like the Lions Club, and even hotel guests and residents. A frequent server was Washington socialite Mrs. Edward Everett (Dolly) Gann, sister of Vice-President Curtis.

The hotel's humanitarian efforts did not end with food. Guests regularly donated overcoats, shoes, and other clothing. More important, some of the noontime diners found jobs through the help of canteen volunteers.

The Mayflower's rescue operation continued into 1931, when Congress (which governed Washington directly at that time) authorized a major public works project for the city, easing the emergency conditions and dramatically shrinking the number of unemployed. The hotel then closed the canteen and concentrated on its own survival.

(opposite) *Mrs. Edward Everett (Dolly) Gann, Vice-President Charles Curtis's sister and official hostess, serving food to the unemployed in the emergency canteen set up by The Mayflower in 1930. At her left is Mr. Daniel O'Brien, manager of the hotel, who initiated the project.*

BUSINESS NOT QUITE AS USUAL

The Mayflower accomplished a lot for afflicted Washingtonians, but it was unable to save itself from the sweeping consequences of the Depression. One of the first symptoms of the national economic downturn was a drop in spending, especially for nonessential travel. Guests were fewer and their stays shorter.

Like so many other American businessmen, the hotel's managers did not realize at first that the Depression would be so severe and would last so long. The Mayflower eventually joined many other U.S. hotels that went into bankruptcy because they could not meet their mortgage payments. In July 1931 its management was taken over by court-appointed receivers, who controlled it until June 1934, when it was returned to its original owner under President Roosevelt's Corporate Reorganization Act.

The Mayflower confronted its economic difficulties with determined optimism and a certain amount of panache. Business seemed to go on as usual, though receipts were down. The hotel retained its cherished high level of service by refusing to reduce its staff, and it continued providing most of the amenities its clientele had come to expect.

Nothing of the hotel's troubles was mentioned in *The Mayflower's Log,* its monthly news and gossip magazine distributed to guests, ex-guests, and a long list of social, professional, political, and business VIPs. Started in the 1920s, the *Log* was half social register and half cultural bulletin, offering articles, short stories, essays, editorials, and vignettes compiled by the hotel's staff. During the 1930s, the magazine virtually ignored the Depression. When it did mention economic conditions, the tone was reassuring—reporting high-level meetings aimed at easing the hard times and profiling guests who had come to Washington to work with President Hoover, and later President Roosevelt, to solve the country's economic problems. But mainly the *Log* focused on the prestigious guests who stayed at the hotel, and on the social events that could distract its readers from the gloomy mood of the times.

MORE PARTIES: THE GREAT ESCAPE

It was, in fact, the Depression itself that inspired some of the Mayflower's most imaginative parties.

In March 1931, the Grand Ballroom was converted into a polo field, with goal posts at each end, spectator boxes on the sidelines, and authentic horse stalls, including one housing a famous U.S. Army polo pony. Placed around the "polo field" were feed boxes, halters, saddles, blankets, buckets, sponges, grooming kits, polo mallets, and other accoutrements of the sport, and many of the guests wore complete polo outfits.

The following year, the Mayflower Garden was transformed into a Spanish cantina, with colorful awnings, geraniums, live parakeets, and other tropical birds. Music for the evening was Latin, mainly tangos and rhumbas—the dance crazes of the time. Hired strollers wheeled carts filled with spring flowers through the crowd, several young men staged a mock bullfight, and all three hundred guests wore Spanish costumes.

Another party, given for President Hoover by Secretary of the Interior Ray Lyman Wilbur, reflected their shared interest in Alaska. For this, the Chinese Room was transformed into an ersatz Alaskan environment with the help of genuine museum pieces. A huge stuffed polar bear on an immense block of imitation ice stood guard at one end of the room in front of two brightly colored totem poles. Evergreen trees completely covered the walls of the room. Hidden among the firs were more stuffed animals—white foxes, a herd of caribou, and a half-dozen American eagles perched on the branches. A replica of Mount McKinley loomed up from the centerpiece at the head table. In the "foothills" were an Alaskan village with Eskimo figures, a miniature railroad running to and from copper mines, and several airplanes—at that time something new in Alaskan transportation.

Perhaps the most elaborate political celebration in the capital during the Depression was the George Washington Bicentennial Celebration, which attracted thousands of visitors to the city. The official ball for the occasion took place in the Mayflower's Grand Ballroom on February 22, 1932. The main event was a pageant in which direct descendants of colonists wore the original clothes of the time, or else faithful copies based on family portraits. One guest was dressed in an exact replica of the wedding gown worn by Martha Custis when she married a tall young Virginian gentleman named George Washington in 1759.

President-elect Franklin Roosevelt being joined by President Hoover for the journey down Pennsylvania Avenue to the Capitol and the official inaugural ceremonies on March 4, 1933.

ENTER FDR

The economic and social climate remained virtually unchanged until the chilly, drizzly, overcast morning of March 4, 1933, when Franklin Delano Roosevelt was sworn in as President. Initially, anxiety hung like clouds over the crowd that gathered around the Capitol to witness the inauguration. Then FDR began to speak in his powerful resonant voice. Words of reassurance rolled out, words he had written the night before at The Mayflower: *"The only thing we have to fear is fear itself"*. The crowd's ovation thundered across the plaza. As he concluded, the sky cleared and sunlight streamed down on the Capital in a seeming miracle that underscored FDR's promise to restore hope and confidence to the nation.

Roosevelt was not a stranger to The Mayflower in 1933. Previously, as Governor of New York State, he had attended President Hoover's dinner for state executives in the hotel. Subsequently, FDR chose The Mayflower again, to take part in a series of conferences on major national and international problems during the Hoover years.

After being elected President in November 1932, FDR chose The Mayflower as the headquarters for his staff of close advisers (popularly known as the "The Brain Trust") and as the living quarters for his family prior to moving into the White House—the only better address in Washington. "We were excited whenever President Roosevelt was coming to the hotel", remembered bellman Reginald Redmond, who was with The Mayflower for more than forty years. "It was always a festive time and we really were on our toes."

President Roosevelt with family members arriving at a dinner for the Woodrow Wilson Foundation, c. 1934.

FDR at a 1934 testimonial dinner for Postmaster General and National Chairman of the Democratic Party James A. Farley. At the President's right is Vice-President John N. Garner; at his left is his son James.

CHAPTER FOUR

Happy Days Are Here Again—The Nation and The Mayflower Change Course

NATIONAL RECOVERY BEGINS

The nation was never the same again after March 4, 1933. True to his inaugural promise, FDR went straight to work on the Depression. Within the first 104 days of his administration—the famous "Hundred Days"—he pushed through Congress fifteen pieces of major anti-Depression legislation. It was an extraordinary achievement for a President in office just three months. Years later, author John Gunther recalled that "almost audibly, a sigh of relief went up through the entire land. . . . FDR blew hope into the deflated body of the country like a boy blowing up a balloon".

The Mayflower offered its own poetic tribute to the President. In *The Mayflower's Log,* the hotel staff mused:

> . . . A few weeks' new Administration
> And lo, a hopeful, trusting nation,

> A people sanguine of all trying,
> Their talk of doing, now, not dying.
> Their faith as strong and firm as granite.
> We might be on another planet.
> A half a dozen months ago,
> All was well and was woe.
> They talked of beer, increased employment,
> But naught but talk is scant enjoyment.
> They tried to dry the farmers' tears,
> Without a thought to tax arrears.
> All life, they said, is a time for grieving,
> This is not a day for disbelieving.
> We must go on, just trusting, hoping,
> Must waste no time in futile moping.
> Then came that Tuesday in November
> A day we always will remember.

NEW DEALERS DESCEND ON WASHINGTON

To Washingtonians, the New Deal quickly came to mean more than a different hand of economic cards being dealt to the country's disadvantaged citizens. Rather, it meant a new tone and mood in their city, which was suddenly inundated by thousands of young people. Fresh out of universities, from law offices, and from Wall Street, these newcomers were drawn by the opportunity to find employment at newly created federal agencies hungry for advice, facts, and statistics. Imbued with social consciousness, intensity of purpose, and an almost messianic zeal, these new government workers created excitement, activity, frustration, and some confusion in the Washington of 1933 and 1934.

Although the natives at first resented the snobbish attitudes of the New Deal crowd, they became grateful for the material benefits that accompanied the change. The creation of thirty thousand new government jobs in Washington thawed the city's economic freeze. With money to spend as a result of pay hikes, government workers now added substantially to the city's commerce and helped create a boom-town atmosphere. Some of their pocket money inevitably found its way to The Mayflower, which was cultivating a

FDR at a banquet in The Mayflower, sitting next to Postmaster General James Farley. At far left is Secretary of State Cordell Hull.

more socially relaxed atmosphere, as Estelle Gaines of the *Washington Times-Herald* observed:

Intensely earnest government girls in budget shop dresses began to appear more and more often in the beautiful Palm Court, where the debutantes and their beaus formerly had the floor to themselves. The G-girls sipped their tea with the "bright young men of the brain trust" who invariably appeared in tweeds or washable suits.

But New Dealers were not only young people. They were also experienced representatives of business and labor, who were drawn into government by such New Deal programs as the National Recovery Administration (NRA). One of these was W. Averell Harriman, board chairman of Union Pacific Railroad, who was to become active in all four of the Roosevelt Administrations, first as assistant to NRA Administrator Hugh S. Johnson, next as a Department of Commerce official, then as lend-lease expeditor-administrator, and finally as U.S. Ambassador to the Soviet Union. During his service to FDR, Harriman lived in the Mayflower's Annex whenever he stayed in Washington.

CONFERENCE AFTER CONFERENCE

The New Deal's explosive activity put the Washington hotel industry back on its feet. Where only months before Washington hotels had blocks of empty rooms, they were now overflowing with guests; some were even forced to send their overflow to boarding-houses. The Mayflower opted to convert forty servants' quarters into guest rooms to accommodate its overload.

Most of the new business came directly or indirectly from New Deal agencies. Because the National Industrial Recovery Act required the framing of economic codes for each major industry in the United States, industry representatives poured into Washington to participate in the deliberations—both to provide expert advice and to protect their industries' interests. At The Mayflower, they attended NRA hearings or gathered to discuss options informally. Attention focused, of course, on the giant iron, steel, coal, oil, lumber, clothing, and textile industries, but the hotel was host also to meetings of many smaller industries. At one time during the drafting of codes, representatives of fifty separate industries stayed at The Mayflower.

Probably the most far-reaching New Deal conference held at The Mayflower was the one sponsored in November 1934 by the Committee on Economic Security to discuss the Social Security program, which Frances Perkins, FDR's Secretary of Labor, declared to be the cornerstone of the Administration's policy. Two hundred experts on social problems were invited to attend. "So great was the interest that those invited not only came but paid their own expenses and bought tickets to a dinner held on the final day of the session", recounted Secretary Perkins. "William Green, president of the American Federation of Labor, indicated in his speech that it was perhaps the most important economic conference ever held in America."

W. Averell Harriman conferri with New York Senator Herbe R. Lehman at The Mayflower.

STAR-STUDDED DIVERSION

Not all was serious business at The Mayflower in the mid-1930s. Show-business celebrities began to appear regularly at the hotel—some as performers, others as guests. Platinum-tressed sex symbol Jean Harlow had made a memorable visit. A Mayflower advertisement tells the story:

THE DAY THE BLOND BOMBSHELL RAN THE SWITCHBOARD AT THE MAYFLOWER

We wish we could say that Jean Harlow was discovered by an eagle-eyed talent scout while she was employed as telephone operator at The Mayflower.

But the truth is, she was famous before she ever visited us. And she, like so many celebrities, heads of state and other distinguished visitors to Washington, chose to stay at The Mayflower.

What set Miss Harlow apart from some of our other notable guests—obvious physical distinctions aside—was her interest and curiosity about the workings of a great hotel.

We found her dining in The Carvery and popping into the kitchen to watch the Chef flambé duck. She had drinks in Town and Country and was generous enough to share her secret for the perfect martini—just a dash of bitters.

But most of all she was fascinated by The Mayflower's switchboard. And she spent the better part of one morning mastering the system, putting orders through to room service and making wake-up calls to people who probably thought they were still dreaming.

Another unforgettable occasion was the guest appearance by one of the 1930s' top radio teams, Amos 'n' Andy. The Mayflower published a promotional ad that read as follows:

WHAT WOULD HAVE HAPPENED TO AMOS 'N' ANDY?

The stage was set for America's two best known comedians to make one of their infrequent appearances at a banquet which climaxed one of the large conventions held in The Mayflower last month.

At the last moment, the toastmaster discovered that his order for a dummy telephone which was to play an important part in the little skit had not been fulfilled by a downtown business firm. He appealed to the banquet manager and the necessary "prop", with an automatic bell, was immediately prepared by one of the house electricians. Andy lifted the receiver and uttered his familiar "Hal-low" without a single member of the distinguished audience being aware of the momentous things that had occurred.

END OF PROHIBITION

A constitutional ban on alcoholic beverages had been voted in the Eighteenth Amendment and enforced through the Volstead Act of 1919. Prohibition, as much a part of the 1920s as bobbed hair and jazz, was more in tune with the spartan values of World War I than with the carefree age of flaming youth. This is, perhaps, why so many Americans opted to vote dry and live wet during the 1920s. Liquor was sold and consumed illegally in huge quantities, both in private and in the countless speakeasies that catered to the popular thirst. By the early 1930s the American public was ready to bring its national laws into line with its drinking habits.

The Mayflower played a role in ending Prohibition by serving as the meeting place of the Women's Organization for National Prohibition Reform. The hotel also was the site of a critical meeting of the Democratic National Committee on March 5, 1931, which was the turning point in the repeal process. At the meeting, John J. Raskob, the committee chairman, broke precedent and insisted that the question of Prohibition repeal be brought into open debate. Party leader Alfred E. Smith, then front-runner for the presidential nomination, supported Raskob's right to the floor. "If the chairman of this committee is to be dragged around because he expressed his opinion, we'd better give up the idea of being Democrats", he said. The *Washington Star* reported, "There were tense moments during the session of the committee yesterday. . . . Wets and drys went at each other in hammer-and-tongs fashion. At times, the uproar in the meeting room drowned out the speaker's words. Hisses and catcalls were heard.". Southern committeemen were so incensed, in fact, that they ultimately abandoned the Smith camp to back the more moderate Franklin Delano Roosevelt. Some historians believe that this defection eventually secured the presidential nomination for FDR.

By the time FDR took office in March 1933, public sentiment was so overwhelmingly in favor of repeal that FDR easily pushed through Congress a bill to legalize alcoholic beverages, beginning with weak 3.2 percent alcohol-content beer, then dropping all limits. Within the year, the Eighteenth Amendment was dead, replaced by the Twenty-third Amendment. Washington and most of the rest of the country (some states passed their own prohibition laws) said goodbye to the speakeasies with their sliding panels, peepholes, and doctored drinks. Beer, wine, and whiskey were legally available for the first time in fourteen long, dry years.

With the repeal of Prohibition, the traditional afternoon tea at hotels went the way of the horse and buggy, and in its place came the cocktail hour. The Mayflower, like other D.C. hotels, quickly paid its thousand dollars for a liquor license. General Manager R. L. Pollio (1932–41) believed repeal was a patriotic gesture, as he eloquently declared only days after legalized drinking returned to Washington:

The return of the accepted complement to civilized dining must instill in all of us a genuine pride in the American people, who, by such overwhelming mandate, decided to close the unfortunate chapter in attempted regulation of personal habits.

We feel that our patrons are now being provided with a service that should have been available all these years. It is with a total absence of paper hats and noise-making devices, but with our new wine cellars bespeaking quality from every shaft, that The Mayflower approaches this return to reason.

OFFICE OF THE COLLECTOR OF TAXES, DISTRICT OF COLUMBIA
RECEIPT FOR
ALCOHOLIC BEVERAGE LICENSE FEE

No 1   Feb. 6, 1934 Washington, D. C., _____ 193__

RECEIVED of The Mayflower Hotel _____ 1127 Conn ave _____
the sum of $ 1,000.00 _____ for a Retailers _____ License, Class C
for a Hotel _____ under the District of Columbia Alcoholic Beverage Control Act.

THIS IS A RECEIPT, NOT A LICENSE
FILE WITH APPLICATION FOR LICENSE

Following repeal of Prohibition, a Mayflower poster announces the opening of a bar, 1934.

Democratic party leader Alfred E. Smith, a strong advocate of repeal, is shown here following a radio program that was broadcast from The Mayflower.

BIRTH OF THE MAYFLOWER LOUNGE

At this time the Mayflower's Palm Court began to flower, serving cocktails and hors d'oeuvres, and catering to those who preferred a lighter lunch than was served in the Presidential Dining Room across the hall. Spurred on by the popularity of the new policy, the Mayflower owners decided to make the Palm Court more up-to-date. They replaced the tropical plants, canaries, and greenhouse charm with a neoclassic, art deco ambiance, hiring New York designer Walter M. Ballard (who created décor for the NBC studios in Rockefeller Center) for the job. With the change came a new name—The Mayflower Lounge—and when the doors were opened in 1934, advertisements called it "a room Washington has waited for since repeal".

The lounge's theme was ancient Pompeii. Featured was a marble fountain and an imposing statue of Bacchus. The color scheme was gold, ivory, and Pompeian red. What gave the room a modern look were the comfortable chairs and couches, a gold sectional carpet that could be rolled back for dancing, and, of course, an elegant bar—twelve feet of solid oak equipped with two handsome beer-dispensing units. It was a busy bar, said the *Washington Times-Herald:* "Waiters scurry about carrying large trays of mint juleps, planters punches, New Orleans fizzes and other warm weather favorites". "The waiters dart through narrow aisles carrying trays of drinks like Albie Booth [1930 Yale halfback] making an end run", added the *Washington Post.*

Not since the early days of Prohibition had Washing-tonians been able to enjoy afternoon and evening dancing in the hotel. Now, once again, couples could swirl around to the music of Sidney Seidenman's Mayflower Hotel Orchestra. "Mr. Sidney" knew everyone's favorite tune and could be counted on to play just loud enough so that dancing and talking could happily coexist.

"Modern but not modernistic. Classic but still comfortable. Every corner reflects a master's hand and insistence on quality. Each piece of furniture was built for a definite place in the room. Aldo Lazzarinni, famed mural artist, was especially brought to Washington to advise in all matters related to color", reported the *Washington Times-Herald.*

With such reviews, it was no surprise that The Mayflower Lounge became "a first stop on any one's social itinerary", according to the *Washington Post.* At the opening festivities on April 2, 1934, seven hundred people crowded into a space designed for one hundred fifty. Each year Washington's elite angled for invitations to the Lounge's Champagne and Orchids Party, which opened the Mayflower's fall social season. Columnist Drew Pearson, radio man Arthur Godfrey, philanthropist Polly Guggenheim, industrialist Walter Chrysler, Jr., Princess Tawhida of Egypt, Alice Roosevelt Longworth (socialite daughter of Teddy Roosevelt), Britain's Lord Louis Mountbatten, and most of the world's famous folk who visited or lived in Washington came to The Mayflower Lounge at one time or another to drink, mingle, and dance.

The Tradition of the Sidneys

A major fixture of the Washington social scene was the music of Sidney Seidenman, violinist-conductor of the Mayflower Hotel Orchestra.

For five decades, beginning in 1926, Sidney—first the father called "Mr. Sidney", later the son—provided dance music as well as concert music for all the Mayflower's public rooms. The crowds and the critics loved "the Sidneys". "Sidney plays such music as makes tears fall in the face of soup", sighed the Washington Star. *"Sidney will strum a solo that will make you fall in love all over again",*

crooned the Washington Times-Herald. *And when The Mayflower Lounge opened in 1934, the* Washington Post *observed, "This is the place to go when you are not sure whether to dance or not. Between dances, the versatile musicians frequently break forth in concert arias. Everyone seems to like it."*

Indeed, the Seidenman style was so popular that in addition to their Mayflower work, the Sidneys often played elsewhere for diplomatic and social gatherings—and even entertained occasionally at the White House.

The Mayflower

announces

Afternoon Tea Daily

in The Mayflower Lounge

Four to Six

beginning Wednesday, the eighth of March

Make Reservations with Eric
District 3000

One Dollar

DINNER DANCES
AT
The Mayflower
7-10 P.M.

SIDNEY AND HIS
ORCHESTRAS

A LA CARTE   NO COVER
SERVICE   CHARGE

In a busy week, Sidney and his orchestra often played at more than a dozen functions. Sometimes a hostess required only a strolling accordionist or violinist. Sometimes a party called for ethnic music—flamenco songs for a "Night in Spain Ball" or Viennese waltzes for a continental-style dance. A highlight among the special engagements played by Mr. Sidney was the Mayflower breakfast for Charles Lindbergh—not only because of its historic importance but because it was Sidney's only booking for six o'clock in the morning. The musicians had finished a

dance engagement late the night before and did not trust themselves to go to sleep before the job; they simply took cold showers, changed their clothes, and went off to play for the hero who had just flown solo across the Atlantic.

Sidney, the father, was known for his distinctive musical style, which combined popular tunes with classics. "He always has the newest numbers, knows the favorite tune of some celebrity, and keeps abreast of current movies and musical shows which visit Washington", beamed the Chanticler Post in 1936. "Last week it was George Gershwin's

Sidney Seidenman, popular leader of The Mayflower Orchestra, c. 1935. "Mr. Sidney" as he was known, memorized the favorite songs of dozens of the hotel's regular visitors.

score from 'Porgy and Bess'. But it could just as easily have been swing music, a Strauss waltz, a Rachmaninoff prelude from Paris." One fan wrote in the Washington Times-Herald: *"I never weary of Sidney Seidenman's music. It strikes me as being about as perfect luncheon and dinner music as could be provided. As an aid to digestion, it runs off the lot any pink pill ever devised."*

Sidney seldom turned down a special request, even if it meant sending someone out to buy sheet music. The Washington Star *once reported:*

A taxi stands waiting his word at The Mayflower door . . . and so the other afternoon when Helen Marye Thomas screamed for "May I" and "She Reminds Me of You" [both from the 1934 movie *We're Not Dressing*] and Sidney had them not . . . he rushed out a music master to that waiting taxi . . . spun him down to a shop and in a jiffy his orchestra was playing "May I".

Some of the occasions for which the orchestra played were bizarre. Clarice Anderson, helper to the Sidneys for

many years, remembered one party thrown by eccentric Mayflower resident Evie Robert to celebrate the birthday of her horse, John the Baptist. Miss Anderson also recalled the time Sidney was asked to fulfill a clause in a will: He played eighteen hours of continuous music before and during the departed's funeral.

Sidney was thoroughly tuned into Capitol Hill. In their Washington Times-Herald column, Drew Pearson and Robert S. Allen recalled that Sidney Seidenman made it his "business to know a man by the music in his soul. Sidney knows, for instance, that Senator James Hamilton Lewis (Illinois) loves to listen to Schubert's 'Ave Maria,' . . . that Representative Florence Kahn of San Francisco is partial to the Blue Danube Waltz . . . Senator Capper, of Kansas, Sidney knows, likes to dance to just a one-step and Senator Millard Tydings (Maryland) wants sophisticated fox trots and waltzes.''.

CHAPTER FIVE

Walking Through the Storm—
The War Years

On Sunday afternoon, December 7, 1941, many Washingtonians were thinking about football. In the last professional game of the season, the Washington Redskins were playing the Philadelphia Eagles. Thousands of people were rooting for the home team at Griffith Stadium; thousands more were riveted to their radios, following every play. Suddenly, news of the Japanese bombing of Pearl Harbor swept through the city in staccato bulletins. The public's attention swiftly shifted from the conflict on the gridiron to the war that had finally come to threaten United States soil. Americans felt menaced—they had to prepare for the contingencies of an enemy invasion, an air strike in particular. There was a real sense of danger pervading the country, especially in major cities like Washington and on the West Coast.

The Mayflower's staff mobilized for the war effort. The day after Pearl Harbor, the hotel's own civil defense organization was created. Its goal was a self-contained system that would enable the hotel to protect its guests during an air raid.

Within one week the plan was in place. The Mayflower's windows and lobby doors were covered with lightproof blinds. The skylights were blacked out. Two air-raid sirens and an emergency first-aid station were installed on each of the hotel's ten floors. The barbershop was stocked with hospital supplies. The roof was turned into a lookout station, equipped with telephones to report sightings of enemy planes, and stocked with firefighting equipment to deal with the effects of incendiary bombing. The *Washington Star* reported, " . . . by the time the war was four days old, the 1,000-room hotel was organized from top to sub-sub-basement, and machinery was set in motion to make it safe without disrupting everyday operations.''.

BEDSPREADS INTO STRETCHERS

Civil defense at The Mayflower directly involved about three hundred of the hotel's eight hundred fifty employees, including chefs, waiters, bartenders, secretaries, and department heads. More than 100 of them registered for Red Cross first-aid classes, and many went on to take advanced training. They learned to turn bedspreads, blankets, sheets, mattresses, and box springs into stretchers; to make bandages from tablecloths and napkins; to transport injured people on tables and chairs; to make emergency use of hotel equipment, such as brooms for splints and bottles of hot and cold water for treatment of shock.

Many employees learned to operate elevators and switchboards so they could take over if it became necessary to alert the guests-or evacuate them in an emergency. Specially trained daytime workers took turns sleeping overnight in a meeting room converted into a dormitory so that someone would always be on hand in the event of a bombing.

The Mayflower's Log, *December 1941: "Roof watchers scan the skies for enemy aircraft. None appear, for this is only a practice alarm. An actual raid would find them prepared to meet all the hazards of civilian bombing."*

Hotel employees enrolled in a first-aid class. The 120 who registered included chefs, waiters, bartenders, secretaries, and department heads.

The Mayflower's Log, *December 1941:* "*'An air raid warning has been sounded in Washington. This is a test.'... Operators repeated this message to hundreds of guests at the start of the capital's first test alarm. Only seven and one-half minutes were required to notify everyone. Supreme Court Justices, Senators, diplomats, and industrialists responded good-naturedly.*"

"*Genial Commodore Longfellow shows his pupils how to make a triangle bandage into a narrow cravat to use as a tourniquet. His patience, wit, and unfailing good humor made him a favorite with Mayflower employees.*"

Guests were expected to do their part as well. Each room was equipped with a blue light bulb (less visible from the air) and instruction sheets for air raids and blackouts. While guests were urged to evacuate their rooms during an emergency, the blackout arrangements permitted hotel activities such as dancing and dining to go on without interruption. To test its system, The Mayflower held a blackout drill, the city's first, on a dark night in February 1942. It was so well executed that the hotel seemed to vanish from Connecticut Avenue. As *The Mayflower's Log* described the event:

One minute the building was its usual glittering self—lights at a thousand windows, guests entering and leaving the main entrance, the doorman's whistle summoning a taxi. Then the wail of a siren was heard, and blackness suddenly shrouded the great facade. A stranger passing the hotel would have thought it an empty office building, if he noticed at all. There was no indication that inside hundreds of guests were strolling in the lobby, dancing in the Lounge, dining as though nothing unusual were taking place.

THIS ROOM

has been

BLACKED OUT

in the event of an

AIR RAID WARNING

tonight

Should you leave
please see that
ALL CURTAINS ARE REDRAWN
and
ALL LIGHTS ARE PUT OUT

DIPLOMATIC AND CULTURAL
LIFE CONTINUES

Despite the wartime conditions, formal dinners, presidential functions, and official parties went on as usual at the hotel. A familiar guest during this period was British statesman Winston Churchill. Some of his visits were private, such as his portrait sittings; others involved official state receptions. Regardless of the occasion, Churchill showed his determination to have a jolly good time. Veteran Mayflower Banquet Manager Walter Seligman recalled serving him at a number of formal dinners. "When it came time for coffee, he always motioned to me and instructed me to fill his cup with brandy instead of coffee." At a later affair in the hotel, when he was Prime Minister, he created a typical Churchillian stir that became the subject of a Mayflower national advertisement:

THE NIGHT WINSTON CHURCHILL PUT HIS FOOT IN IT AT THE MAYFLOWER

Churchill was seated across from FDR at one of those open oval tables they use for State Dinners. It was directly under the dome in our red and gilt Chinese Room. The dinner was proceeding very properly. But after dessert was served, Churchill leaned toward a friend at his right and whispered a "wonderful Winnie" joke in the man's ear. Two distinguished ladies gasped. Conversation stopped. And a flush rushed up President Roosevelt's starched white collar. Sir Winston's unrepeatable remark had become tomorrow's talk of the town. It was the dome: making the same awesome echo you hear when you say your name ever so softly in the Capitol rotunda. Now we never put people with secrets to tell in the Chinese Room. We couch them in a candlelit corner of the new La Chatelaine, where strolling minstrels keep conversation strictly tête-à-tête. And we save the Chinese Room for anyone who wants his words to ring down through the years.

Volunteers donating blood for the war effort in a special room set up in The Mayflower.

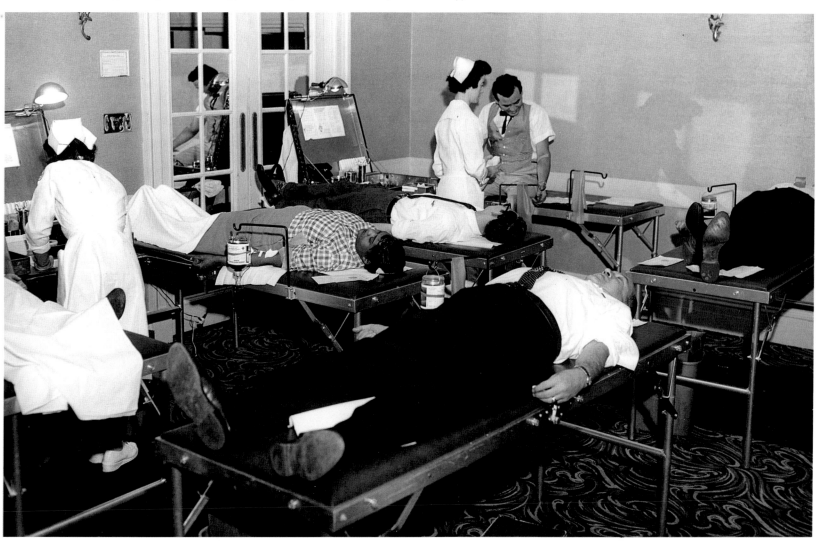

The night Winston Churchill put his foot in it at The Mayflower

Churchill was seated across from F.D.R. at one of those open oval tables they use for State Dinners. It was directly under the dome in our red and gilt Chinese Room. The dinner was proceeding very properly. But after dessert was served, Churchill leaned toward a friend at his right and whispered a "wonderful Winnie" joke in the man's ear. Two distinguished ladies gasped. Conversation stopped. And a flush rushed up President Roosevelt's starched white collar. Sir Winston's unrepeatable remark had become tomorrow's talk of the town. It was the dome: making the same awesome echo you hear when you say your name ever so softly in the Capitol rotunda.

Now we never put people with secrets to tell in The Chinese Room. We couch them in a candlelit corner of the new La Chatelaine, where strolling minstrels keep conversation strictly tete-a-tete. And we save The Chinese Room for anyone who *wants* his words to ring down through the years. Which room may we save for you?

STATE DINNER
WINSTON CHURCHILL
FRANKLIN D. ROOSEVELT
MARCH 4, 1946

HISTORY IN THE MAKING *The Mayflower*

(opposite) *Mr. Mack greets Prime Minister Winston Churchill as he arrives for a stay at the hotel.*

The Duke of Windsor signs the Mayflower guest book, while the Duchess, left, and Margaret Hart (Canby), society editor of the Evening Star, *look on. The famous couple were at the hotel for a tea party hosted by the American Newspaper Women's Club, c. 1945.*

Another much-publicized visit was the arrival of the Duke and Duchess of Windsor for a tea hosted by the American Newspaper Women's Club. "The occasion was completely informal, and the Duchess lived up to her reputation for soignée", reported Betty Hynes in the *Washington Times-Herald*.

Pencil slim, the Duchess could dare to wear a peplum in front of her black gown. She surrendered the familiar beanie for a spray of magenta bird of paradise on her hat, that matched her short gloves. Her patent leather pumps had closed toes, and she wore a diamond pin, and a black and white pearl earring mounted in diamonds. . . .

During the party a waiter approached the Duke and said, "We have been instructed to serve you at your table." "Thank you", he said, "but we prefer to mingle among our guests." And so they did, giving a thrill to many. . . .

While the seal of Great Britain hung on the great mirror over the mantelpiece [in the East Room] . . . , we are convinced that dearer to Wally's heart was the confection concocted by Fred [Wiesinger, the hotel's maître d'], which included both the Seal of the Free State of Maryland and the Royal Lions of the United Kingdom. The Duchess drank innumerable sips of coffee, and the Duke was fascinated by the lighted fountain of punch that dispensed intriguing amber liquor all during the party.

Some of the more memorable presidential affairs at The Mayflower were Franklin Roosevelt's birthday galas. "The President swept in like a potentate", remembered bellman Reginald Redmond. Each year on January 30, FDR celebrated his birthday by holding a series of balls to raise money to fight polio. (Polio was an unpreventable disease until 1953 and FDR himself was one of its victims.) These balls, held at Washington hotels, were front-page news from coast to coast and attracted stage, screen, and radio stars who wanted to contribute to the cause. At The Mayflower one year, Mickey Rooney took over the drums for a few hot licks; another year Ginger Rogers swirled around the Ballroom stage. One year Al Jolson was master of ceremonies, and another year it was Guy Lombardo.

Warbling cowboys Gene Autry and Roy Rogers came to the FDR balls, as did leading ladies Rosalind Russell, Betty Grable, Ava Gardner, Ruth Hussey, Loretta Young, Lynn Bari; leading men Jimmy Stewart and William Holden; and comedians Jack Benny and Harpo Marx.

Even when FDR could not attend, the fund-raising balls went on. In 1943, while the President was away on a secret war-strategy mission, thousands jammed local hotels to celebrate his sixty-first birthday. The *Washington Star* reported:

Evidence that the dancers were thinking of the President as they celebrated his birthday was given at The Mayflower last night, when the crowd cheered long and loud as comic Lou Costello . . . shouted, "Nobody knows where he is, but he's *here,* brother". . . . Charlie McCarthy, complete with top hat and tails, helped Mrs. Roosevelt blow out the 61 candles. . . . Everywhere the stars outdid themselves to entertain the dancers. Dennis Morgan sang. Abbott and Costello mugged. James Cagney went into a dance. Laraine Day recited the closing speech delivered by Joel McCrea in the movie "Foreign Correspondent", while Edgar Bergen and Charlie McCarthy wisecracked, and Roy Rogers sang and played his guitar.

Gloria Jean and Mickey Rooney at an FDR Birthday Ball.

THE MAYFLOWER AS MUSE

Grand hotels have always held a great fascination for those hoping to see someone famous, powerful, or exciting. In hotel lobbies and public rooms, travelers without a pedigree or fame can rub elbows with the titled, statesmen, movie stars, artists, writers, and other celebrities. And the privacy of hotel rooms surely conceal lovers' illicit rendezvous, business plots, and political jiggery-pokery.

Hotels hold so much potential for tantalizing intrigue that they are often used as settings for movies. The most famous of these was the 1932 Metro-Goldwyn-Mayer film *Grand Hotel*. Ten years later a Paramount picture called *Remember the Day* used The Mayflower as one of its main settings. The film, starring John Payne and Claudette Colbert, intertwined a story about a presidential campaign with an elderly schoolteacher's reminiscences about her students. Many of the scenes were shot in the hotel's lobby, flower shop, Promenade, and upstairs hallways. The film's political rallies were replications of the Mayflower's real-life campaign parties and inaugurals.

The Mayflower's ambiance and historical tradition attracted many kinds of artists—painters, writers, musicians, photographers, performers. For some, the hotel was a backdrop for their work. For others, it was a home.

Illustrator Norman Rockwell sketched around the bustling wartime lobby in preparation for a series of Washington paintings that eventually appeared in the *Saturday Evening Post*. Film director Howard Hawks spent two weeks at The Mayflower collecting material for the movie *Air Force*. Columnists Drew Pearson and Neil Vanderbilt regularly used The Mayflower as a listening post. Some artists took up residence in The Mayflower, developing or finishing projects during their stays. In the early 1940s, John P. Marquand was frequently seen sitting quietly in The Mayflower Lounge during the months it took him to write two of his novels: *So Little Time*, published in 1943, and *B. F.'s Daughter*, published in 1946. In *B. F.'s Daughter*, much of the action takes place at The Mayflower, and the novel gives the reader the feel of hotel life dur-

Claudette Colbert in stills from the 1942 film Remember the Day, *shot largely at The Mayflower.*

ing the War. In one passage, the main character makes this vivid observation:

The fifth floor smelled of a violent antiseptic which the hotel had taken to using. It had been done over shortly before the war by a New York decorator in a dashing, modernistic manner. The carpets were swirls of black and green, and the chairs and sofa by the elevator, done in white leather, looked like things she had seen in her solid geometry book at Bryn Mawr. The corridor was vibrating with the beginnings of Saturday night. As she followed the bellboy, she saw tables on wheels outside of doors, and she heard humming voices. The door next to the suite that Tom had managed to get for them was open as she passed, giving her a glimpse of officers and girls, smoking, laughing and sitting around tables covered with ginger ale bottles. As she walked by the open door while the boy was working with the key, she had time to see that the officers were young, and she could see by their baggage that they must have come from overseas.

Norman Rockwell, whose ''Four Freedoms'' paintings were familiar to millions during the War, was frequently seen in the Mayflower lobby studying types for a series of Washington sketches that appeared in The Saturday Evening Post.

Television journalist Edward R. Murrow gives a talk in one of the hotel's meeting rooms.

Several portrait painters set up elegant studios at The Mayflower to make their subjects feel at home. Among them was Douglas Chandor, whose portrait of Winston Churchill was declared by the Prime Minister—a painter in his own right—to be a masterpiece. Chandor also painted Franklin Roosevelt and Herbert Hoover as he sat in a Mayflower armchair.

If they were not actually working or living in the hotel, many artists enjoyed being part of the Mayflower's lively environment. A partial list includes composer George Gershwin, writer W. Somerset Maugham, cartoonist Peter Arno, playwright Noel Coward, guitarist Andrés Segovia, journalist Walter Lippman, conductor Leonard Bernstein, humorist Ring Lardner, ballet director Rebekah Harkness, violinist Isaac Stern, painter Henri Matisse, conductor Arturo Toscanini, and at least four Nobel laureates—Sinclair Lewis, Sigrid Undset, Rabindranath Tagore, and Thomas Mann.

THE WAR GOES ON . . .

Washington after Pearl Harbor became a city bursting at the seams. The war brought in thousands of new workers, and this runaway growth taxed the city's services. There were long lines everywhere—at the movies, in restaurants, at bus stops, and at Union Station. Everything was at a premium. Housing became so scarce that a one-room apartment that had gone for $55 a month in 1940 cost $625 a month in 1942. Hotels, too, felt the pressure. As the *Washington Star* reported, "Washington hotel managers have seen the value of a room soar in public estimation to the level of diamonds, tires, and other priceless possessions.".

At a time when housing was the scarcest commodity in Washington, C. J. Mack, the Mayflower's general manager, kept the hotel's ethical standards high. He ignored the profiteers who came to the hotel flaunting fifty-dollar bills and Capitol Hill connections to obtain or hold onto scarce rooms. He resolved that the hotel would cater principally to those who were vital to the war effort, and he had his own highly placed government contacts to determine whether a particular guest's presence was important or not. For those the government needed, the hotel made its rooms available indefinitely; for those deemed peripheral to the war effort, the hotel strictly enforced an official five-day limit.

English artist Douglas Chandor with his portrait of President Hoover. Mr. Chandor finished the painting while in residence at The Mayflower, 1931.

Former President Herbert Hoover breakfasting in his Mayflower suite with Secretary of Agriculture Clinton Anderson, c. 1943.

The 1940 painting, "The Signing of The Constitution of The United States", was unveiled in the rotunda of the Capitol. It was painted by Howard Chandler Christy, who lived for a long time in The Mayflower.

According to The Mayflower's Log, *1931, "This remarkable unposed picture was snapped in the main lobby by Dr. Erich Salomon, who is a world-famous photographer. Neither Arturo Toscanini (right), conductor of the famous New York Philharmonic Symphony, nor his friend, Maurice Van Praag, were aware of the photographer's presence. Dr. Salomon caught Mr. Van Praag in a gesticulative pose . . . in a picture made only a few hours after Conductor Toscanini had made an appearance in Washington."*

Spanish guitarist Andrés Segovia shown here in his Mayflower suite while in Washington to perform with the National Symphony Orchestra, c. 1946.

As a result, the character of the Mayflower's clientele changed dramatically from the prewar years. John P. Marquand wrote about the besieged hotel: "The elevator, like the lobby, was overstuffed. When [a woman] entered, the men took off their hats, but they all shoved past her when they got out. Washington was no longer any place for a lady." Socialites, tourists, and wealthy visitors from abroad were generally less in evidence than were government officials, men in uniform, and military contractors.

Celebrities continued coming to the hotel, but only on war business. Playwright Thornton Wilder did special work for the Army Air Corps; humorist Irvin S. Cobb sold war bonds; and cartoonist Walt Disney was busy creating his own army of small creatures in support of Uncle Sam. Army and Navy relief benefits and war bond campaigns brought to the hotel some of movieland's brightest stars—Dorothy Lamour, Groucho Marx, Gene Kelly, Claudette Colbert, Joan Fontaine, Olivia De Havilland, and Erroll Flynn. Some stars who stayed at the hotel were in uniforms themselves: Tyrone Power (Marine), Robert Montgomery (Navy), Frank Capra (Army), Clark Gable (Air Force).

Walt Disney in his hotel suite, c. 1942, warning Mickey Mouse to beware of the cat.

MAKING DO IN WARTIME

Mayflower Manager C. J. Mack was creative in his efforts to help the many visitors who regularly traveled to Washington on wartime government business. These people often arrived in the early morning only to find that their rooms were not yet vacated or their reservations not yet confirmed. To relieve the discomfort and inefficiency of this situation, Mack established the Interim Club.

The Interim Club was no makeshift locker room. Designer Dorothy Draper was commissioned to convert former bedrooms on the hotel's second floor into comfortable temporary quarters, complete with private closets, dressing rooms, showers, tables and desks, lounging chairs, telephone booths, and two attendants. The club allowed guests to freshen up, change their clothes, do paperwork, make phone calls, and receive messages and telegrams before their scheduled appointments. There was no charge for these facilities.

Mr. Disney discusses his forthcoming movie, "Victory Through Air Power", with Clare Boothe Luce in the May-flower lobby.

Two photos from the Evening Star, *February 6, 1942. The caption reads: "Interim Club for Businessmen—These out-of-town businessmen, here on defense work, can find a place to clean up at The Mayflower Hotel before going out on appointments."*

Humorist Irvin S. Cobb said, "I consider myself one of the country's unsolved problems, so I've come to headquarters." While staying at The Mayflower, Mr. Cobb sold war bonds.

At another wartime fund-raiser Van Johnson, Judy Garland, and Eddie Bracken stand at the banquet table.

Actor Brian Aherne boosting wartime morale during a crowded party in the Grand Ballroom.

Comedian Red Skelton shakes hands with General George C. Marshall. Mrs. Marshall looks on.

Gene Kelly entertains a packed Grand Ballroom during a war bond benefit, c. 1942. "Mr. Sidney" is conducting the band.

A USO dance at The Mayflower.

The Mayflower tried to maintain as high standards in feeding its guests as it did in housing them. Shunning tempting black-market dealings, the hotel bought its produce and other foodstuffs only from legitimate, government-regulated suppliers. So, like the rest of the country, The Mayflower had to contend with shortages of meat, sugar, butter, and oil, not to mention haute cuisine ingredients such as caviar and truffles. Chef Nicholas Marchitelli and his staff spent much of their time planning menus that would provide good dining with the available foods. In the process they developed original dishes with inventive substitutions, such as using black olives instead of the usual truffles on a Mayflower specialty dish.

Staffing was, of course, a continual problem, since the armed forces drafted all but the oldest of the hotel's able-bodied men. It became necessary to hire almost all new workers—many of whom had backgrounds and qualifications only distantly related, if at all, to the jobs for which they were hired. For instance, when the position of night auditor became open, the applicants included a photographer, an embalmer, a machinist's helper, an inventor, a furrier, and an electrician (who got the job).

"DESTINATION—THE MAYFLOWER. WANT A RIDE?"

Sharing was the idea behind another Mayflower initiative during the war. Because the military needed all the metal, rubber, and gasoline it could get, private cars and fuel in the nation's capital were almost as scarce as housing. Most people going to work had to jockey for standing room on overcrowded streetcars and buses. To help this situation, Mr. Mack encouraged those Mayflower employees who had cars to give rides to people headed in the direction of The Mayflower. The staff responded handsomely, putting printed signs on their windshields that said, "Destination—The Mayflower. Want a Ride?"

The Mayflower helped the war effort in many other ways. It sponsored bond drives and volunteer recruitment campaigns in the lobby, gathered books to be sent to the armed services, and turned over its billboards to patriotic messages. It urged guests not to use the telephone during peak business hours; it sent furniture to the Kiwanis Military Camp in Hawaii; and, to honor those Mayflower employees who left their jobs to fight for their country, it displayed commemorative plaques in the hotel lobby.

The habits of Washington society were changed dramatically by the war. Executive clubs gave up annual banquets; individual debutante balls and formal evening wear were dropped. Almost no one held large private banquets, and many socialites arrived for small dinner parties boasting: "I came by bus!" Although the upper crust had to endure these social limitations, they were, on the other hand, able to enjoy the company of scores of foreign officials and distinguished expatriates who came to Washington as refugees from the Nazis.

This international mix had some drawbacks, however. Because the conversation in Washington hotels so often dealt with war matters, there was concern in

An invitation to The Mayflower Lounge's "Fall Opening" party to raise money for the Stage Door Canteen.

A Mayflower billboard supporting the war effort.

THE MAYFLOWER ROLL OF HONOR

IN TRIBUTE TO THOSE EMPLOYEES WHO HAVE LEFT THE STAFF OF THE MAYFLOWER TO ENTER THE ARMED SERVICES OF THE UNITED STATES OF AMERICA, WE RESPECTFULLY DEDICATE THIS TABLET AND INSCRIBE THEIR NAMES BELOW

ACTON, RAYMOND L.	LAIGNEL, WILLIAM
ADAMS, NORWOOD	LA RICOS, JOHN
ARRINGTON, THOMAS	LLOYD, EDWARD G.
BODKIN, EARL	McHUGH, FRANK
BOVARD, GRIER C.	MARGELOS, PETE
BROWN, AUBREY R.	O'CONNOR, ANDREW W.
CACCAVO, EDWARD	OVERTON, LAWRENCE S.
CARRIERI, MAURO	PRATT, WILLIAM B.
COFFMAN, C. DeWITT	RICE, MENDELL F.
COSIMANO, FRANK	ROBERTS, OSGOOD
CUTLER, WALLACE M. Jr.	ROOT, FRANCIS A.
DINTAMAN, CHARLES D.	SHEA, WILLIAM E.
DURAN, JULIO MORALES	SHERMAN, NORBERT F.
ELDRIDGE, ROBERT	SULLIVAN, JOHN T.
FRANCIS, AUGUSTUS	SUTPHIN, ELVIN T.
GAMEL, L. DEXTER	TEMPLE, GEORGE J.
GEBICKE, JULIUS B.	VACCAREST, HENRY C.
GLEIM, HOWARD R.	VALENTINE, VERNON
HALL, ROBERT I.	WATHEN, THOMAS
HEWITT, HERMAN H.	WILSON, ARTHUR G.
HILDEBRAND, RICHARD V.	YOUNG, N. FERRELL

Commemorative plaque in the hotel lobby with the names of employees who volunteered for the armed services.

the government that official secrets could find their way across tables and into the wrong ears. Against this danger, the Justice Department issued an order to ban German, Italian, and Japanese aliens from employment at all hotels. The Mayflower complied and had to drop twenty-five waiters. As an additional measure to discourage loose talk, The Mayflower placed on every table a card that depicted Hilter, with gargantuan ears, saying, "Go on and talk . . . I'm all ears".

THE WAR IS OVER

The Washington Stage Door Canteen in the Belasco Theater was made possible by actress Helen Hayes. She helped raise money to convert the performance space into a social and recreational facility where men and women from all branches of the military could forget their troubles for a few hours. One of the fundraisers for the Canteen was the Blackout Ball at The Mayflower. Another was the Champagne & Orchids Party in The Mayflower Lounge—a traditional event for the hotel that was held in 1943 for the exclusive benefit of the Canteen. Senator A. B. "Happy" Chandler of Kentucky, Washington hostess Pearl Mesta, and film star John Boles were among the guests who paid the $1,000 cover charge for the evening. The rules were strict at the Canteen: no kissing and no dating the young hostesses, who were there to dance with the soldiers.

There was one night, however, when everyone broke the rules: August 14, 1945, the day the war ended. As news of the victory reached the Canteen, there wasn't a hostess who wasn't being kissed by a man in uniform. Everyone in the Canteen—as well as the swelling crowds in the streets—released the emotions they had pent up for almost four years. The people of Washington danced, tooted automobile horns, clanged streetcar bells, exploded firecrackers, and laughed and shouted. On sidewalks carpeted with confetti, servicemen were mobbed by civilians wanting to hug them, kiss them, and shake their hands. In the hotels, people formed parades and walked around singing. The *Washington Times-Herald* described the night as "the wildest, noisiest, most joyous and most colorful" the capital had ever known, with "one solid mass of waving, weaving, screaming humanity". The war was over.

Copies of this card were placed on the hotel's tables to remind people to speak discreetly regarding war information.

Senator A. B. "Happy" Chandler singing "My Old Kentucky Home" at the Champagne and Orchids evening in The Mayflower Lounge in 1943.

Attending that same event was Washington hostess Perle Mesta who, along with Senator Chandler and the other guests, paid $1,000 each to help the Stage Door Canteen. Here Miss Mesta is shown with Mrs. Oscar Chapman, left, and Mrs. Vinson, widow of the Supreme Court Chief Justice.

The Mayflower Lounge opened in 1934. Earlier the room was called the Palm Court, and had a quiet ambience of tropical plants and birds. Now its interior was filled with lively dance music and a large oak bar serving alcoholic beverages (after years of Prohibition). Seen here in the late 1930s, The Mayflower Lounge was described by the Washington Post as "a first stop on anyone's social itinerary".

Doorman Bob Beaver at the Connecticut Avenue entrance.

CHAPTER SIX

Good-bye Elegance, Hello Efficiency—The Postwar Years

SERVICE REACHES A PEAK

In 1948, *International Steward* magazine asked C. J. Mack, general manager of the hotel, what secret formula The Mayflower used to keep its traditional standards so consistently high. Mack pointed to the staff.

Fred Wiesinger, our maître d'hôtel, is in a class by himself. He represents the fine old school of the restaurant profession which is built on generations of training (in Austria he served the house of Hapsburg). "Mr. Fred", as he is affectionately called by thousands of our patrons, symbolizes the difference between guessing and really knowing. Others of the staff who have given The Mayflower the reputation it enjoys are: Nicholas Marchitelli, chef de cuisine; Max Steiner, banquet director; Mario Palmieri, chef confiseur; Anthony Marcello, chef grand mange—all of whom have been with The Mayflower since its opening.

Because of the unique character of life in the national capital, the demand for elaborate entertaining is more constant than in most cities, so the staff never has a chance to get out of practice. It is not unusual for The Mayflower to serve 15 to 20 large parties a day.

Two others typical of the exceptional people who have served the hotel for long periods are waitress Virginia Falta-Lee and doorman Mike Mann. At this writing, Falta-Lee is seventy-nine years old and has been with the hotel for thirty-four years. "Moving between tables in her thick-soled black oxfords, [she] is an inconspicuous living legend at The Mayflower Hotel", wrote Lucy Keyser in the *Washington Times*.

Chef de cuisine Nicholas Marchitelli (for whom the Nicholas Restaurant was named) carves a Christmas turkey.

The Mayflower's much respected maitre d'hotel, "Mr. Fred" Wiesinger, standing by one of the lavish banquet tables for which he was famous.

Mr. Fred.

One of the Mayflower's collection of paintings at the De Sales Street entrance.

One of the hotel's three paintings of the ship Mayflower *by James G. Tyler. This one shows John Alden, Priscilla Mullens, John Carver, William Brewster, and Miles Standish in the foreground.*

One of the Commonwealth seals in the East Room.

Gilded capitals along the upper walls and recesses of the Promenade.

Frieze of classical allegorical figures at the east end of the Promenade.

President Truman, with CARE volunteer Mrs. Edward L. Emes, signing up as the first donor to the "CARE Dollar Day Drive". Each dollar contributed sent a 22-pound surplus food package to the needy overseas.

A proud waitress attends to President Harry S. Truman, c. 1950.

President Truman at a press interview in the hotel.

William (Mike) Mann opened doors for the hotel guests for forty-two years. He arrived at The Mayflower two days before it opened in 1925 and never missed a day of work. Although a Russian who couldn't read or write English, he made a fortune through stock tips from Mayflower guests, particularly George Romney, then president of American Motors. When he died, Mann left $100,000 in stocks and savings to ten Washington-area charities.

THE TRUMAN EXPERIENCE

In 1948, Harry Truman, the incumbent President, was beginning his race against Republican nominee Thomas E. Dewey. The press predicted that Dewey would win easily, as did nearly all the political pundits. Truman begged to differ. At a Jackson Day dinner in the hotel's Grand Ballroom he told a doubting audience that he would beat Dewey: "I want to say that during the next four years there will be a Democrat in the White House—and you're lookin' at him". Truman's self-confidence did not alter the negative press coverage of his campaign. On election night, newspaper headlines called Dewey the winner. But the next morning, the country learned that Truman had made good on his prophecy in one of the most dramatic upsets in U.S. history. He was soon to celebrate his victory with a joyous inaugural dinner at The Mayflower.

Throughout his term in office, Harry Truman made The Mayflower one of his favorite places for mingling with friends and strangers. So doing, he won the hearts of the Mayflower staff. Down to earth and without guile, he genuinely liked people and made friends easily. The public always felt close to the man who thought of himself as an ex-haberdasher as much as President. Truman would turn up unannounced at the hotel, walk up to statesmen and doormen alike, slap them on the back, and say "Good morning" or "Nice to see you". A generous man, he liked to give his favorite hats to friends and to write personal thank-you cards and checks to waiters and other hotel staff. After one party in 1958, the former President sent a five-dollar check to each waiter and a ten-dollar check to banquet manager Walter Seligman. Not one of these checks was cashed; they were valued much more as mementos than as money. Indeed, Seligman wondered how Truman would ever be able to balance his checkbook.

Even as a vice-president, Truman made a strong impression on the Mayflower staff. Bandleader Sidney Seidenman, Jr., carries a letter in his wallet that his father, the hotel's original maestro, wrote to him when he was in the Army in World War II. The letter recalls an evening Sidney senior had shared with Truman. "I played a dinner the other night in honor of Vice President and Mrs. Truman", the letter begins. "He played piano with us (The Fairy Waltz, Chopsticks, etc.), and it was very cozy. He seems a very swell guy. I don't suppose the German vice-presidential equivalent would go around playing with the likes of me, now would he? That could only happen here and damn few other places."

Truman had originally planned to stay in Washington following his presidency and live at The Mayflower. Suite 676 was reserved for him and renamed

The Connecticut Avenue facade.

the Presidential Suite. But when his intended Democratic successor, Adlai E. Stevenson, lost his bid for the presidency, Truman changed his mind and decided to return to his home town of Independence, Missouri. In 1953, however, about four months after he left office, Truman did stay for a period at The Mayflower.

By that time everyone on the staff recognized the ex-President on sight—everyone, that is, except one innocent new employee. According to a Mayflower advertisement headed *The day the Mayflower cashier wouldn't give Truman credit:*

She was a sweet young thing, new to the city and new to her job as cashier at The Mayflower. In the town she came from people didn't meet history book heroes in the flesh, so when the former President came to check out, it never crossed her mind that he could be THE Truman. So she asked to see his credit card. He didn't have one. So she said

she'd call the Credit Manager (that's Mayflower procedure). But she smiled when she said it (that's also Mayflower procedure). And the credit manager explained to her gently that Presidents of the United States don't need cards.

No, she didn't get fired. Instead she had her picture taken with Mr. Truman. As for Mr. Truman, he was delighted to receive the privacy and anonymity that famous people yearn for but rarely get.

When he finally settled his account, Truman asked a Mayflower bellman to ride with him to Union Station in a White House limousine with flags flapping on the fenders. After the ex-President got his bags checked in, he gave the bellman a big tip and told the chauffeur to drive him back to The Mayflower—a thrill the bellman never forgot.

It is hard to imagine the Truman brand of informal personal contact being used by a President in today's supertight security conditions.

THE MAYFLOWER GETS HILTONIZED

In 1947, hotel magnate Conrad Hilton made national headlines when he paid $2.6 million for a controlling interest in The Mayflower Hotel. Despite objections from a minority group of stockholders, who said they had been forced to accept less than market value for their stock, Hilton's purchase was declared legal and he proceeded to put the Hilton stamp on The Mayflower, his fourteenth hotel.

Having sailed ahead for two decades through rough and calm seas in the grand tradition, The Mayflower now faced an abrupt shift in course. After a war that had significantly reshaped the country's economic and social structure, the United States was making the difficult adjustment to peacetime conditions. Returning veterans and other Americans were busy rebuilding their lives. As postwar prosperity grew, more and more people were on the move, eager—and having the means—to travel for both business and pleasure. They would want comfortable rather than elegant lodgings when away from home, reasoned Hilton. And so he set about remodeling The Mayflower to appeal to vacationing families and to the growing convention business.

The gold leaf in the Ballroom, the brocade curtains, the silk-upholstered furniture, and period furnishings—none of these old-world touches seemed right to Conrad Hilton. Nor was the art-gallery look of the Promenade, with its fine cloisonné and tapestries woven by old masters of Aubusson. The Promenade's three main sculptures were sold to National Memorial Park Cemetery in Falls Church, Virginia. The gold leaf, so lauded in the hotel's opening years, was covered over with paint. And *The Mayflower's Log,* the

monthly publication sent to the hotel's blue-ribbon clientele and members of the press for decades, was discontinued. For many people who had experienced the hotel's prewar glory, the Hilton years were a disappointment. It was as if an elegant ocean liner had been converted into a no-frills ferryboat.

Nowhere was the transformation more dramatic than in The Mayflower Lounge. In the summer of 1947, nearly every bit of ornamental plaster was removed from the walls and ceilings. The walls were painted in shades of gray to give the room a modern, neo-industrial appearance. Gray fiberglass drapes were added, and a ten-foot-high upholstered leather screen was placed across the alcove to the east. Four murals, by French artist Jean Pages, were commissioned to depict the Capitol, the Washington Monument, and the Lincoln and Jefferson memorials.

These changes should have brought cheers; instead they drew groans and criticism. The reaction moved Mr. Hilton to approach his next remodeling with more attention to design. In 1950 The Mayflower Lounge was done over in Georgian style, in shades of rose. Unfortunately, the original murals were painted over. The west end of the room was raised to give guests a view of the stage, a chandelier was added, and a service door was cut in the southern side of the west wall. This design was more happily received. According to columnist Harry MacArthur:

Conrad Hilton, the man who also bought The Mayflower, can come back now. All is forgiven. Veteran inhabitants of The Mayflower who snarled bitterly when Mr. Hilton went to vast expense to undecorate their favorite rendezvous a

Sports stars Sonny Jurgensen, Jim Kaat, and Pete Gogolak at The Mayflower in the early 1970s. Doorman Bob Beaver is at right.

couple of years ago, can have nothing but high regard for him today. . . . Georgian influence, chandelier, sconces and all, the major achievement of this redecoration of The Mayflower Lounge is the creation of a warm, informal atmosphere in informally elegant surroundings. . . .

Soon the lounge was as busy as ever, which was very, very busy.

The new Hilton Mayflower was designed to appeal to a faster-moving, less sophisticated clientele. Automatic elevators were installed, as were trendy gift shops, a modern drugstore, and air conditioning throughout the hotel. The main dining room, newly wired with Muzak, was the Rib Room, a busy restaurant designed to cater to the tastes of the increasingly mobile groups of Middle Americans who stayed at the hotel. Not surprisingly, the Rib Room featured steaks, prime rib, and chateaubriand. The Town and Country dining room replaced the original 1920s drugstore. The remodeled hotel was, in general, efficient and popular, with more families and conventioneering guests than ever before. Despite the invasion of the hoi polloi, the blue-chip guests continued to come— probably because the Mayflower staff never stopped giving first-rate service.

Left to right: Col. Henry Crown, vice president of Hilton Hotels; Mr. Conrad Hilton, president; Associate Justice of the U.S. Supreme Court Thomas C. Clark; and C. J. Mack, the Mayflower's general manager. Conrad Hilton was guest of honor on the occasion of the hotel's twenty-fifth anniversary party, February 21, 1950.

THE HOTEL'S SILVER ANNIVERSARY

In 1950, three years after he took over the hotel, Conrad Hilton threw a newsmaking party for one thousand guests to celebrate the twenty-fifth anniversary of the Mayflower's opening. He also invited more than a dozen employees who had been with The Mayflower from the beginning.

"The conversation piece at this party was the 56-foot table set up in the ballroom and loaded with suckling pigs and turkey, frogs' legs, crown roasts, seafood Newburg, pâtés, glacés, ice cream, and cakes", noted the *Washington Post*. "A sunken garden coursed its way down the center of the table, tubs of white azaleas, silver leaves, and feathery ferns taking on a blush pink tone from the indirect light. Small tables ringed the room; Sidney and his orchestra played, and every guest stopped to view the chef-d'oeuvre, the culinary masterpiece, which was a book page reproduced from Hilton's biography, *The Man Who Bought the Waldorf,* only here it was rendered in sugar on a gold standard."

This National Geographic Society photo was taken at the Daughters of the American Revolution Convention in 1951, in the Mayflower's "Hiltonized" Grand Ballroom. The photo's caption reads: "With Music, Flags, and Flowers, 1,500 Daughters and Guests Say Good-by until the Next Year—The President General, her cabinet, past Presidents General, and other national officers sit at the speakers' long table . . . Music is by the United States Marine Band."

Convention's Work Is Done; 1,500 Daughters and Guests Relax at the 1951 Banquet
During most of the Congress, delegates carry on daily sessions, committee meetings, elections, and genealogical searches. Here they enjoy the fruits of their labors.

With Music, Flags, and Flowers, the Daughters Say Good-by until the Next Year
The President General, her cabinet, past Presidents General, and other national officers sit at the speakers' long table in Washington's Mayflower Hotel. Music is by the United States Marine Band.

The *Washington Times-Herald* reported:

What caused all the visiting hotelmen—and there were many of them—to exclaim and point their fingers excitedly, were the decorations in the glacé—the colored shells of gelatinous substance that covered much of the cold food. Little motifs of leaf and blossom were repeated again and again with the bit of off-symmetry characteristic of hand-painted

china. Those little flowers were handmade. The leaves were bits of cucumber rind. The red petals were from parings of radishes. And again and again on the platters, as side decorations, were red and white roses. They were carved from beets and white turnips. . . . The kitchen staff had been working on it since Friday [five days]. It looked as if it had taken a month.

EISENHOWER AT THE MAYFLOWER

Some of the "Ike" years were the calmest in recent history. The Korean War was over, no one had heard of Vietnam, and President Eisenhower could concentrate on problems at home. In 1953, Eisenhower's first year in office, a special event was held in his honor. Columnist Barry Gray recorded it in the *New York Post* as follows: "It was a moment before the hour-long TV show [produced by Rodgers and Hammerstein] was to begin. Lucille Ball and husband Desi Arnaz had flown in from Hollywood; Ethel Merman from Denver; Eddie Fisher, Jane Froman, Lilli Palmer, and Rex Harrison from New York. Just before the President entered the Mayflower dining room, the most resplendent assortment of bigwigs I've ever seen took their places of honor." The occasion was B'nai B'rith's Anti-Defamation League dinner for Eisenhower, who came to the hotel to accept the League's Democratic Legacy Award for his role in ending segregation in the Army.

This tribute was appropriate for the man who also attended Presidential Prayer Breakfasts at The May-

flower with his Vice-President, members of the cabinet, the Supreme Court, and often as many as ninety senators and three hundred congressmen. These breakfasts were probably the closest the hotel came to holding joint sessions of Congress.

These were also the years of the McCarthy reign of terror. The Wisconsin senator himself threw an all-night party at The Mayflower for more than a hundred "anticommunist" guests. From midnight until dawn they consumed eggs, beef, and three kinds of melon, washed down with large quantities of liquor and wine.

Meantime, Ike entertained special guests at the hotel. At one dinner in honor of King Saud of Saudi Arabia, a pond was installed for the occasion, complete with lilies and goldfish. At another official reception, this one for Indonesia's President Sukarno, a veteran banquet captain accidentally stepped on Ike's foot. The President reassured the embarrassed captain. "Don't worry", he said. "A lot of people have stepped on my toes before."

President Eisenhower strides through the Promenade en route to the dining room to attend the televised ceremony honoring him for ending segregation in the Army.

President Dwight D. Eisenhower making an address at the hotel shortly after his election in 1953.

Conrad Hilton welcomes the President of the United States to his hotel, c. 1954.

President and Mrs. Eisenhower pose for photographers at the State dinner for President Sukarno of Indonesia, 1954.

AN UNFORGETTABLE OCCASION

One of the most talked about parties at The Mayflower was given in 1953 for the capital's diplomatic corps. Marie McNair of the *Washington Post* observed, "Washington hasn't seen anything like last night in a long time. And, most guests admitted, it would be a long time before it happens again.". She was referring to the white-tie reception and buffet supper in the Grand Ballroom and Chinese Room given by General Rafael Trujillo, then dictator of the Dominican Republic.

In attendance that night at the reception, which followed the ceremonial signing of a mutual defense-agreement between the United States and the Dominican Republic, were Central American diplomats, U.S. congressmen and senators, members of the Supreme Court, and ranking State Department officials.

The receiving line was in the Chinese Room. McNair continued, "Necks stretched, eyes popped as guests took in the giant bouquet of American roses on a center table . . . the dozens of vases filled with delicate spring flowers . . . the Dominican and American flags side by side (both red, white, and blue) . . . champagne bubbling from lighted fountains."

(above) *General Raphael Trujillo, the Dominican dictator, with his son and an aide as they enter the Grand Ballroom, 1953.*

(left) *Trujillo chatting with guests at his white-tie reception.*

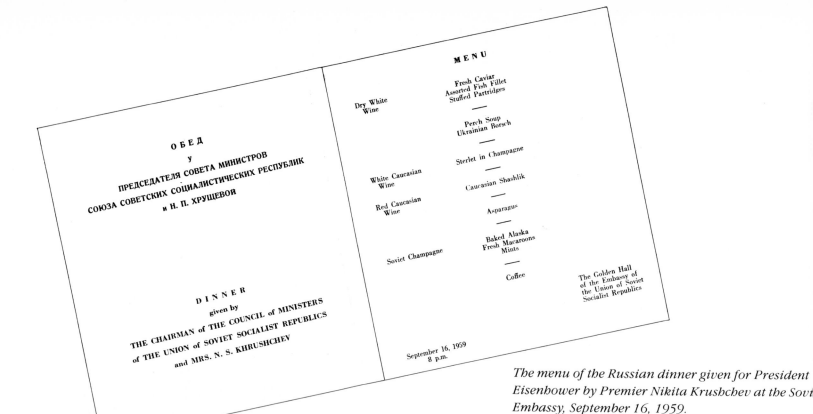

The menu of the Russian dinner given for President Eisenhower by Premier Nikita Krushchev at the Sovt Embassy, September 16, 1959.

Three pieces from the hotel's gold service showing the stamp of the ship Mayflower *and the hotel's name.*

One of The Mayflower's gilt-edged plates, reserved for the most formal occasions. When not in use, the gold service is stored in the hotel's vault.

Bring Out the Gold

Nineteen fifty-nine saw the first U.S. visit of a Soviet head of government in decades, and President Eisenhower ordered the White House's gold service brought out for the occasion. When Premier Nikita Khrushchev reciprocated with a dinner at the Soviet Embassy, he had a problem: All the Soviet gold was in Russia, and it would hardly do for the embassy to borrow the gold service from the White House. So the Soviet Union established "diplomatic relations" with The Mayflower—the only other facility in

Washington with gold service. Within hours the gold plates came out of the Mayflower vault to carry the specially imported food: hot smoked Russian sturgeon, Beluga caviar, and baked Alaska (Khrushchev's favorite dessert). The hotel also provided gold-braid uniforms for the extra help needed to cater the party.

The entire event was coordinated by the hotel's Larry Wiesinger (son of Fred, the maître d') who was subsequently thanked by the Russians with a box of Beluga cav-

Standing near the banquet table is the Mayflower's Larry Wiesinger (son of "Mr. Fred"), who coordinated the event for the Soviet Embassy and supplied the hotel's gold service. Note the larger-than-life portraits of Lenin and Krushchev.

iar. Recalling the event years later, Wiesinger said, "The dinner was a friendly act. It was something we were happy to do for our country."

The Mayflower's brilliant gold-plated flatware, gilt-edged china, and glassware has been used in state functions honoring the King of Thailand, President Charles de Gaulle, the Shah of Iran, King Saud, Queen Elizabeth, and other heads of state. The gold service also includes épergnes *(fruit stands)*, candelabra, and vases, as well as a three-piece gold plaque with matching épergnes *made by Thormire, goldsmith to Louis XVI. (About 1815, Lafayette bought a matching set and presented it to First Lady Dolly Madison. This set is still in the White House.)*

When the Grand Ballroom was opened for dinner, Sidney Seidenman's Mayflower Orchestra greeted guests as they made their way to the fifty-foot table, shimmering with the gold service. It held pheasants in plumage, lobsters piled high, salmon in aspic, roast Vermont turkeys, fillet of beef, black beans and roast lamb, pâté de foie gras, salads, chocolate mousse, and ice cream smothered with crushed strawberries. This was Mr. Fred at the top of his form.

Trujillo was remembered at the hotel for his ostentatious spending. "He was the biggest tipper I ever had", recalled Mayflower doorman Mike Mann. "He would tip a hundred dollars every click of the heels."

THE HOOVER-CHAPMAN CONNECTION

Longtime FBI director J. Edgar Hoover ate lunch at The Mayflower almost every working day for two decades, starting in 1952. Sitting in his personal corner (where, in true crime-fighting style, he turned his back to no one), Hoover almost invariably ordered the same meal: chicken soup, buttered toast, and a salad of lettuce, cottage cheese, and grapefruit. Waiter Joe Chapman served him during the last eight years of his life, and the two developed a genuine friendship. Hoover would send Chapman postcards from his travels.

"He always brought his own diet salad dressing because he was trying to lose weight", recalled Chapman. "Sometimes he'd forget it, and then I'd have to run out and get the jar in his limousine."

Hoover's Mayflower luncheons became so well publicized that when reporters wanted to find him, they scouted the hotel's main entrance and lobby, sometimes forcing him to slip out through the kitchen to avoid them. But Hoover also did some scouting of his own. According to a 1950s *Mayflower's Log* article:

THE DAY J. EDGAR HOOVER CAPTURED
PUBLIC ENEMY NO. 3
DURING LUNCH AT THE MAYFLOWER

Mr. Hoover was enjoying his customary luncheon . . . when between bites he noticed the third most-wanted man in the country just two tables away.

With his usual unruffled dispatch, he had the man arrested and taken away. Mr. Hoover resumed his meal. And he returned to The Mayflower again the next day, just as he did almost every weekday for more than 20 years until his death.

This luncheon ritual was so much a part of Hoover's routine that when the movie *The Private Files of J. Edgar Hoover* (1977) was being cast, Waiter Chapman was hired to play himself in the daily scenario on camera and also to coach starring actor Broderick Crawford on how to portray the FBI chief with authenticity—at least during the lunch hour.

Chapman was so fond of Hoover that when "The Director" died in 1972, the waiter draped his special table in red, white, and blue bunting, and refused to allow anyone to sit there until Hoover was buried. For years after, curious FBI cadets came to the hotel just to cast their eyes upon the famous Hoover corner.

FBI Director J. Edgar Hoover, with an aide, Mr. Tolson, carefully examines the menu of the Mayflower—though it is well known that Hoover ordered the same lunch nearly every day for about twenty years and sat at the same table.

Hoover's favorite waiter, Joe Chapman, instructs actors Broderick Crawford (playing Hoover) and Dan Dailey on how to eat lunch at the Director's regular table during the filming of The Private Files of J. Edgar Hoover *on location in The Mayflower, 1976.*

COLONEL SANDERS SAMPLES THE POULET

Kentucky Fried Chicken, that staple American two-legged fast food, started with a bang in the 1950s. White-haired Colonel Sanders, its founder, was a national celebrity when he arrived at The Mayflower in 1959. His first dinner was a major event for the hotel's cooking staff. It was remembered in a Mayflower promotional piece:

THE DAY A FAMOUS KENTUCKY COLONEL ORDERED FRIED CHICKEN AT THE MAYFLOWER:

The gentleman is somewhat of a rare bird—a self-made success in the fast food field. We considered it an honor and a privilege to serve him.

However the event was not without its tense aspects. The Colonel, true to his reputation, ordered poulet fricassée, putting us much on our mettle. For even though we have had kings, queens, heads of state and other noteworthy personages as guests, serving someone his own specialty is something of a challenge.

In short order, the moment of truth arrived. The waiter proudly presented the Colonel with his meal—the aforementioned bird, petit pois de jardin, salade vert and an unpretentious yet amusing glass of wine.

The suspense was unbearable. The Colonel inhaled the rapturous aromas arising from his plate. Brandishing his utensils with supreme skill he delicately separated a tender morsel and conveyed it to his mouth. He smiled. "This heah bird is fingah lickin' gooooood", he said.

Mr. Hoover at the 1964 dinner given in his honor by The Women's National Press Club in the Grand Ballroom. At the podium is Miriam Ottenberg, prize-winning reporter for the Evening Star.

HILTON FORCED TO UNLOAD

The success of Conrad Hilton's expanding hotel empire in the 1950s had an ironic backlash—the loss of The Mayflower. The Justice Department's antitrust division, charging that Hilton was monopolizing convention business in New York, Washington, and several other cities, required him to sell off some of his properties. In 1956 he sold The Mayflower for $12.8 million to the Hotel Corporation of America (HCA). At the helm of HCA, which later became Sonesta International, was A. M. Sonnabend, a hard-driving executive who made his reputation and his millions by revitalizing an assortment of businesses.

HCA quickly put into motion its own plans for modernizing The Mayflower. It did away with the upholstery and silver shops, which had maintained the hotel's fine furniture and silver collection. HCA then removed what was left of the original Promenade, covering the rough plaster walls with vinyl and selling off additional artworks, including a hundred-year-old sculpture of Pocahontas that went to a collector for his garden in Sorrento, Italy. HCA remodeled the lobby, enclosing the mezzanine-level balcony and its graceful wrought-iron railing in order to create new office space. The relief sculpture on the eastern wall was covered, and the overhead sunburst medallion was hidden by a dropped ceiling. The new owners threw out the ornate pier capitals, replaced them with marble tiles, and covered the walls with walnut-veneer box paneling and vinyl.

HCA cut back both staff and equipment in the kitchens, making food preparation less labor-intensive and more automated. It also did away with the fashionable Mayflower Lounge, bringing the curtain down on one of the nation's most beloved listening posts; the lounge disappeared behind green and white doors to become a new restaurant—first the Presidential Dining Room and later Le Châtelaine.

Most of Washington society abhorred these changes, especially the loss of The Mayflower Lounge, but the remodeling of that particular room into a dining area actually added to the Mayflower's luster in one important way. It gave the hotel two fine landscape murals by Edward Laning, best known for his murals in the New York Public Library and on Ellis Island. The paintings, each about twenty-five feet wide and fourteen feet high, depict formal gardens with pools, fountains, topiary arches, stone cherubs, urns, balustrades, and steps leading off into a romantic distance. Other nice touches were added, such as sixteenth-century-style carved-oak Spanish doors and Gothic-style oak paneling for the Rib Room.

Generally speaking, however, HCA, like Hilton before it, contributed little to the hotel's luster. In fact, stripped of its patrician trappings, The Mayflower started to founder. In the 1960s and 1970s it lost much of its fashionable image and traditional atmosphere. Writing in the architectural publication *Skyline,* July 1985, Charles Lockwood observed: " . . . the passage of time did not lessen the convenience of its location on Connecticut Avenue, midway between the White House and Dupont Circle. Nor did the years destroy its magnificent architecture. All The Mayflower needed to blossom again was a top-to-bottom renovation and an upbeat new spirit." And that's exactly what it got.

Sweet Victory and Sour Defeat

Jubilant inauguration balls at The Mayflower have a long tradition, but even more a part of the hotel's life is the drama of presidential election nights. Campaigners struggle for many months for victory at the polls, pinning their dreams—sometimes their careers—on that one day in November. The nation's two major political parties often have made The Mayflower their election headquarters at the same time and have held their election-night vigils side by side; by evening's end, the victory of one side adds poignancy to the defeat of the other. When, for example, the

Eisenhower camp cheered its victories in 1952 and 1956 at The Mayflower, the supporters of Adlai E. Stevenson—also headquartered there—disbanded in heartbroken disappointment.

When the tide was turned in 1960 and the Kennedy Democrats won the race, a teary Richard M. Nixon arranged a private thank-you party for his staff at The Mayflower. Earlier that same election night, some of the ten-thousand Democratic celebrants at The Mayflower ran amok; they took doors off hinges, pulled metal room num-

Democratic Presidential candidate Adlai E. Stevenson getting encouragement from Rhode Island Senator Theodore F. Green in the Mayflower lobby, 1952.

enator George McGovern, the unsuccessful Democratic andidate for President in 1972, and his wife celebrate Christmas 1985 at The Mayflower. Here they are inspecting one of the many Christmas trees that line the Promenade.

Sad news is announced in the Grand Ballroom as Stevenson loses to Eisenhower in the 1952 election.

bers off doors, and raced up and down the hotel's hallways yelling out the latest returns to some very disgruntled, awoken guests. "Democratic supporters, intoxicated with the scent of a victory, whooped and hollered wild cries of support last night, as Senator John F. Kennedy's lead mounted . . . ", reported UPI. "Screams of 'We want Jack' echoed down Connecticut Avenue outside The Mayflower where Democrats threw an open house. . . . " About 11 P.M. Kennedy rooters broke into an uproarious songfest in The Mayflower ballroom, chanting, "California Here We Come", "Swanee", "Anchors Away", and other popular melodies.

But a bitter Republican shocked hotel employees and guests alike even more than did the ecstatic Kennedy camp. The next morning a bellhop found, deeply scratched in six-inch-high letters on the polished wood top of an antique table, the word NIXON.

Concierge desk in the Promenade.

STILL THE HOTEL OF PRESIDENTS

Through all the infelicitous remodelings and alterations inflicted by successive owners, The Mayflower continued to be host to the most important residents of Washington.

In January 1961, with the elegance and grace that was her hallmark, Jacqueline Kennedy made her debut as the nation's First Lady. Looking like the legendary snow queen in her sparkling white chiffon sheath and gossamer cape, she greeted thousands of Democrats who came to The Mayflower to celebrate her husband's inauguration as the thirty-fifth President of the United States.

It was a day few Washingtonians would forget. Just hours before the ball, a blizzard had draped the city with a twelve-inch mantle of snow, hampering every kind of travel. Understandably determined to attend the festivities, President-elect Kennedy exercised a presidential prerogative prematurely by ordering official transportation from the White House. It was a wise decision, for there was not a rentable limousine or taxi to be had in the twenty-four hours before and after the inauguration. (Mayflower doorman Bob Beaver recalls Texas oilman H. L. Hunt offering $150 to anyone who could find him a taxi—but even at that price there was none available.)

Not many celebrants were eager to leave The Mayflower that snowed-in night; most were relieved to be able to stay overnight at the hotel. Fortunately, the Kennedy staff had set aside a block of one hundred rooms for such personal friends as Pierre Salinger, Senator Jacob Javits, Pat Boone, Jack Paar, Elizabeth Arden, Dorothy Kilgallen, and former President Harry S. Truman.

The evening festivities climaxed a long day for John and Jacqueline Kennedy. In addition to the inaugural balls held at five different Washington hotels, there had been a celebratory luncheon earlier that day at The Mayflower, given by Joseph Kennedy, the President's father, for two hundred Bouviers, Auchinclosses, Lees, Kennedys, and others related and close to the First Family. The famous Kennedy wit flourished at the luncheon. At one point John Kennedy was asked to defend his choice of brother Robert F. Kennedy as Attorney General. "He's got to have some experience before he practices law", the President quipped.

Former President Truman at a Mayflower reception with President Kennedy, Vice-President Johnson, and Speaker of the House Sam Rayburn, on March 10, 1961.

(opposite, left) *John and Jacqueline Kennedy in front of one of James G. Tyler's paintings of the ship* Mayflower.

(opposite, right) *President Kennedy arriving at the hotel for a State dinner given in his honor by Vice-President and Mrs. Chen of the People's Republic of China, August 2, 1961.*

A dinner honoring Kennedy was given by President and Mrs. Houphouet-Boigny of the Ivory Coast Republic, May 24, 1962.

Informal lounge and cocktail area in the main lobby.

View of the lounge and reception area, looking east through the Promenade.

Lounge area in the Promenade.

Seventeenth Street entrance—the east end of the Promenade.

President Kennedy making a speech at a May-flower function, c. 1962. Left to right are Vice-President Johnson, Senator Carlson, and Mr. and Mrs. Billy Graham.

Mr. Kennedy leaving The Mayflower. Senior Doorman Mike Mann, who worked at the hotel for forty-two years, at left.

Attorney General Robert Kennedy speaks in the Grand Ballroom. To his right is Supreme Court Chief Justice Earl Warren, c. 1962. Commissioner Duncan of Washington is at far left.

At the 1965 inaugural ball at the hotel: President and Mrs. Lyndon Johnson and Vice-President and Mrs. Hubert Humphrey.

Reception area and entrance to the Nicholas Restaurant.

Several years later, in 1965, Lyndon Johnson's Vice-President, Hubert Humphrey, on the occasion of the hotel's fortieth birthday, sent a telegram that expressed his personal thoughts about The Mayflower: "I feel like an adopted member of the hotel since I have, over the years, eaten so often in the Rib Room, spoken so often in the meeting rooms, and, of course, lived so well there with my family during inaugural week. . . . I send my thanks." Three years later, during his campaign for the Presidency, Humphrey invited 162 Delaware delegates and Democratic officials, with their spouses, to a reception at The Mayflower. According to the Associated Press, "He wined and dined them in candlelight and to music, had singer Nancy Sinatra and basketball star Elvin Hayes there to sign autographs—and made one of his shortest speeches on record, fourteen minutes. . . . The women were given charm bracelets and the men tie clasps bearing the vice-presidential seal."

Vice-President Lyndon Johnson in January 1962 presenting a testimonial plaque to John B. Duncan for his service as Commissioner of the District of Columbia. The sponsoring organization was The Big Brothers of the nation's capital.

Johnson and Humphrey conferring at The Mayflower with Senator Walter George of Georgia, c. 1966.

Vice-President Humphrey being congratulated after a banquet speech by Hotel Manager C. J. Mack, c. 1968.

President Johnson at a Mayflower reception for President Park of Korea, c. 1967.

Honesty Pays Off for Hotel Maid

From the Fort Worth (*Texas*) Mind, *May 10, 1962:*

Early last month a happy traveler boarded a plane at the National Airport here for New Orleans, and his happiness was the kind you feel when you discover in your fellowmen whose traits most of us cherish: kindness, honesty and neighborliness.

In his pocket this traveler had $900 he wouldn't have had

but for the honesty and integrity of Mrs. Daisy Higdon, a maid at The Mayflower Hotel where the visitor had stayed.

A careful man, our unknown traveler had tucked his bankroll—$921—under his pillow when he went to sleep.

In the morning he wasn't so careful; he dressed, grabbed his briefcase, and went about his business, leaving the money behind.

President Johnson greeting King Hussein of Jordan at the hotel's main entrance, c. 1965.

And there Mrs. Higdon found it when she came in to make up the guest's room, just where he'd put it for safe-keeping the night before.

And safe it was, for Mrs. Higdon turned the whole wad over to Housekeeper Catherine Witherall who, in turn, saw that the guest from Louisiana got his money back.

In gratitude the guest rewarded Mrs. Higdon with a double sawbuck from his recovered wallet, and the hotel, proud of Mrs. Higdon's part in sending the guest home happy, added a $25 U.S. Savings Bond to the reward.

It was a good day for traveler, maid, and hotel—and is the kind of story to warm anybody's heart.

CHAPTER SEVEN

Restoration Sets The Mayflower Back on Course

$\mathcal{I}n$ 1966 it took only $14 million to purchase The Mayflower, just $1.2 million more than HCA had paid for it a decade earlier. Some observers thought that even this was no great bargain, for The Mayflower in the mid-1960s seemed to have a far brighter past than future. Other people thought differently. Four of them banded together to form May-Wash Associates, and soon The Mayflower had a new set of owners. For the first time since its earliest years, the owners of the hotel were local Washingtonians who had an abiding interest in the landmark and what they saw as its potential. They also had direct personal ties to the hotel when it was in its heyday.

Kingdon Gould, Jr., a descendant of the powerful nineteenth-century financier Jay Gould, and onetime Ambassador to the Netherlands, was the only one of the four owners who, as a young man, entered and left The Mayflower by the front door. William Cohen had once been a D.C. trash collector whose customers included The Mayflower. Dominic Antonelli, as a young man, had been a parking-lot attendant for The Mayflower. And Ulysses Auger had been a busboy at The Mayflower in the 1930s and was forever in awe of the clientele of those prewar years.

During the Depression, these men (teenagers at that time) started their business careers in the Washington area. Antonelli bought a small lot, and Auger had a carry-out restaurant on 22nd Street, where he and Antonelli frequently would lunch together. William Cohen regularly stopped there for breakfast on his daily trash-truck route. Over the years the three became

good friends. As the city grew, so did they. Auger opened more restaurants, Antonelli opened more parking garages, and Cohen built up a fleet of trash collection trucks.

After World War II, each of the future partners began to invest in real estate. Soon their entrepreneurial paths crossed, and they began investing together in larger ventures. "Everything was done by a handshake", recalls Auger. "If we knew you were good for it, we did business with you. If you weren't, we walked away." According to Auger, William Cohen called him up and offered him a share of the partnership. With his acceptance, the ownership group became complete.

For William Cohen, the catalyst for the transaction and the majority owner, purchase of The Mayflower represented the high point of his career. He referred to the hotel with delight and excitement, and considered it to be the jewel of his real estate holdings. When he died in 1973, his son Richard continued his interest in the hotel. For him, also, "The Mayflower is a once-in-a-lifetime project". This sentiment is echoed by Antonelli: "It's a landmark in my life"; and Auger, too, is jubilant about the special place The Mayflower holds in his life.

The decision to revitalize The Mayflower made by the four partners became official in January 1981, when Kingdon Gould, Jr., told the press: "As owners, we are committed to the idea that The Mayflower Hotel must continue to be a significant asset to the city, and we will maintain for many years to come the standard of excellence for which it has been famous."

Business partners and good friends, from left to right: William Cohen, Dominic Antonelli, Kingdon Gould, Jr., and Ulysses Auger. In 1966, these four purchased The Mayflower and later decided to restore it to its original glory. Behind them is the original scale model of the Mayflower *ship.*

THE NIXON INAUGURAL

Band leader David Remington of Rockford, Illinois, entertained at Richard Nixon's inaugural ball at The Mayflower in January 1969. Remington recalled: "When we got up there about 10:30, I hit that mob with the fact that it was Illinois that put Nixon over the top, and we ripped into the 'Illinois Fighting Song'. It tore the place apart. I spotted Senator Everett Dirksen and got him up to sing 'My Country 'Tis of Thee' and 'God Bless America' and he left to an improvised 'When the Saints Go Marching In'." Dirksen was such a hit that many newspaper accounts said he nearly upstaged the President.

By the time Nixon arrived, sometime after midnight, many of the three thousand celebrants were sagging. The crowd jammed, jostled, and pushed, with no room for dancing. But the new President, still in good spirits despite the day's exhausting events, managed to pep up the throng once again. He said that his predecessor, Dwight Eisenhower, confided that he ordered his tickets for the ball eight weeks ago. "I told Ike that I had made my reservations eight *years* ago", Nixon said.

Mrs. Nixon wore a mimosa-yellow double-faced silk and satin gown with a richly beaded jacket said to have taken 260 hours to embroider. "She probably was the most elaborately dressed First Lady at an inaugural ball in modern times", speculated Ymelda Dixon of the *Evening Star*.

During his long association with the hotel, Nixon was most remembered as being the last to leave any Mayflower party or meeting, and for nonstop talking. He was nicknamed "Bucklejaws" by the hotel staff and security guards.

President and Mrs. Nixon welcome France's President Charles de Gaulle at a formal function at The Mayflower, c. 1970.

The Worst Easter in History

The late 1960s were frightening times for Washington. Not even the grande dame *of Connecticut Avenue could escape the racial upheavals. During the rioting, burning, and looting that followed the assassination of Dr. Martin Luther King, Jr., in April 1968, the capital was turned into an armed camp patrolled by nearly 14,000 national guardsmen and 1,400 policemen. It was the most severe disturbance in Washington's 168-year history—leaving 8*

dead, 987 injured, more than 4,600 facing police charges, and millions of dollars' worth of property damage.

On what would ordinarily have been a jubilant and busy pre-Easter weekend, downtown stores were closed and sidewalks deserted except for soldiers on guard at key posts. A curfew was strictly enforced. "The usual vast springtime tourist invasion has become a trickle in the heat of racial violence in the nation's capital, leaving the city's

The Nixon inaugural ball, January 1969.

leading industry reeling in what should have been the rich-est week of the year", said the Associated Press. Hard hit were hotels, restaurants, and bus tours, as visitors in town for the canceled Cherry Blossom Festival fled the city. Most Washington hotels, including The Mayflower, reported that they were less than 25 percent occupied.

The only open restaurant at The Mayflower was the Cof-fee Shop, and it was having trouble keeping up with cus-tomer demands. In his article "Washington Is a Different City", John R. Cauley of The Star vividly recalls the scene:

I got to The Mayflower Hotel and looked into the lobby. About five persons were there. We entered and found the coffee shop open—finding a place to eat in Washington is difficult now—but there was only one waitress trying to serve twenty hungry customers, most of them obviously

THE CHINA CONNECTION

In February 1973 President Nixon had arranged for the United States to exchange diplomatic missions with the People's Republic of China. When the Chinese delegation arrived in the United States, however, their two Embassy Row buildings were still being refurbished and were nowhere near ready for occupancy. After several fruitless attempts to find temporary quarters for the Chinese diplomats, the White House called upon The Mayflower.

Although the hotel was in the midst of one of its busiest conventions—the annual meeting of the Daughters of the American Revolution—General Manager William Hulett juggled the room assignments until he found a satisfactory way of housing the Asian dignitaries, most of whom did not speak English. They were moved into a suite of twelve rooms on the sixth floor, complete with phone lines to Beijing. At first there were only ten delegates, but the number soon swelled to thirty-five as spouses, cooks, and office help arrived. And the planned two-week visit grew into an eight-month stay. The Mayflower recorded their unique residency in a promotional ad:

THE DAY THE MAYFLOWER MET CHINA
ACROSS THE TABLE. AND LOST:

. . . Understanding how important it is for guests to feel at home, one of the first things we did was present them with a ping-pong table. Then we challenged them to a friendly game . . . and lost. So, we decided to stick to our own game . . . service and hospitality.

This time we met our Chinese friends on our own ground. We went to work and helped the delegation unravel the hundreds of complexities of a new life in the nation's capital. Their friendliness and cooperation made the project a genuine pleasure.

The Chinese, most of whom had not been out of China since 1939, needed lots of help in adjusting to the modern American way of life. One of their needs was automobile transportation. An assistant manager of the hotel volunteered to help by arranging the purchase of a Cadillac through a car dealer he knew. The dealer was not inclined to do business with the "Red Chinese", so a car was eventually bought from a Buick dealer. Returning to The Mayflower with a grand limousine, the young assistant manager raced up to the delegation's suite, eager to take the proud new owners for a drive. However, they asked only to have the car pointed out from their sixth-floor window. Upon seeing the wondrous machine, the chief delegate grinned and said, "It's beautiful, please buy six more." Unfortunately, there is no record of the first dealer's reaction upon learning that he had lost the sale of not one but seven Cadillacs. And, true to their reputation for loyalty, the Chinese Embassy still buys its cars from Ralph Brown, the same Buick dealer.

The Chinese traditionally prefer their native food, and these diplomats were no exception. To oblige, The Mayflower, on six days each week, brought in chefs from local Oriental restaurants—first Trader Vic's, later the Yenching Palace—to cook and serve Chinese lunches and dinners for the delegation. On the seventh day, they ate American food.

A close bond developed between the Mayflower staff and the Chinese. "They're really very nice", one hotel employee told columnist Jack Anderson. "They appreciated service, and they showed it by giving us small gifts—just simple things, like folding fans and scrolls, but it shows they care about us", the employee continued. "And they don't forget their [American] security guards. One night they gave a special

stranded tourists. . . . By 9:30 the lobby was deserted. We could not help but think if there had been no riots, the place would have been jammed with tourists here for the Cherry Blossom Festival.

The turmoil eventually subsided. But as the Washington Post *remarked, "It isn't any secret it's something that will*

take time to recover from.". Guests and organizations, some reflecting the era's newly expanded social consciousness, returned slowly to The Mayflower. Among them were Business Executives Move for Vietnam Peace and Catholics Against the Ban on Birth Control. There was also a foodless banquet to call attention to, and raise money for, the starving children in Biafra.

dinner for the security people just to thank them.''

When the new Chinese Embassy was finally ready in late 1973, The Mayflower threw a Wild West farewell party for the delegation in the State Room, providing the delighted but nonplused Chinese delegates with cowboy hats, boots, neckerchiefs, sheriff badges, and a screening of cowboy movies—an extraordinary cross-cultural experience for the Chinese. At the end of the party General Manager Hulett presented the delegation with a replica of the *Mayflower* ship. The Chinese reciprocated with a painting of panda bears. As a further gesture of appreciation, Hulett was invited to visit China—an offer he happily accepted the same year.

On October 19, 1973, Henry Kissinger was greeted by Huang Chen, Chief of the People's Republic of China delegation, at their temporary quarters at The Mayflower. A two weeks' stay was planned, but the Chinese remained guests of the hotel for eight months, until the Chinese Embassy was ready for occupancy.

When the Chinese delegation was ready to leave The Mayflower to occupy their new Embassy, General Manager William Hulett presented to Ambassador Han Hsu a scale model of the ship Mayflower *as a farewell gift. The presentation was made at a Wild West Party, complete with cowboy hats, country music, and horseshoe pitching, arranged by The Mayflower on November 30, 1973.*

During the farewell party, the staff and members of the Chinese delegation played ping-pong. Staff member Barbara Hulstrom watches Frank Glaine wait for the serve.

Bob Beaver holds the door for Big Mac in November, 1972. The 1,600-pound steer is believed to be the largest guest in the Mayflower's history. He resided, briefly, in the hotel's Promenade doing his best to lobby for legislation against importing beef.

Steering for Publicity

The following article by Louise Lague appeared in the Evening Star, *November 28, 1972:*

Nobody could believe it really, when Big Mac came right through the front doors of The Mayflower Hotel yesterday and walked up to the registration desk in search of a room.

Not one to argue with a 1,600-pound steer, the desk clerk filled out a registration form and assigned Big Mac to the first floor promenade. As one Mayflower employee said, they couldn't give him a room because "he's just too big for the elevator".

Big Mac is The Mayflower's largest guest ever, but he's not here to sightsee. He came with 170 livestock owners from the Midwest and West who want to talk to Department of Agriculture officials about meat prices and why they are rising. The owners want to work out a system of grading meat and educating the public about which cuts cost more and why.

But nobody was talking business yet when Big Mac got himself settled in the corridor yesterday afternoon. Several sheets of plastic, plywood, and a bale of hay were laid out on The Mayflower's fancy red rug, and Mac was penned in with a portable fence.

Big Mac was totally unimpressed by the mirrored walls and crystal chandeliers, said Wayne Otte, who accompanied the steer in his van all the way from Red Oak, Iowa.

But the hotel staff was impressed by Big Mac, and so were the hotel guests and the rest of the citizenry who came in off the street to see what that steer was doing in The Mayflower.

More than just a curiosity, Big Mac is a steer with a story. Although he is pure-white French Charolais, his first owners dyed him black last summer to enter him in the National Western Stock Show in Denver. Disguised as an American Angus, Big Mac took the grand championship.

McDonald's Hamburger Systems immediately snapped the steer up for $14,250 only to discover that Big Mac was white at the root.

The Denver District Court returned the money to McDonald's, who sold Big Mac at auction to Eddie Collins of Red Oak, who is an agricultural writer and broadcaster.

Collins decided to take Mac on a publicity tour of the East to protest federal government action in increasing meat import quotas.

THE PRESIDENTS KEEP COMING

While Nixon's inaugural ball of 1969 was marked by traditional protocol and formal attire, a very different tone was set at The Mayflower eight years later, in 1977, when thirty-five hundred "down-home folks" danced the Carter Administration into office. The excited and partly denim-clad crowd cheered "Yes!" when Jimmy Carter asked them if they would support him in the next four years. And they roared when he asked, "How do you like my wife's old dress?"—it was the same light-blue chiffon frock Rosalynn had

worn to his inauguration as Governor of Georgia in 1970. The Carters then took a spin around the dance floor while their daughter Amy watched from the sidelines, clutching a bouquet of miniature roses and peeping out from behind her large horn-rimmed glasses. The *Baltimore News American* reported: "From Carter's enthusiastic, almost adoring reception, it appeared that those who supported him throughout his long quest for the presidency still felt he was Jimmy and not Mr. President."

Young Amy Carter is the momentary center of attention at her father's inaugural ball, January 20, 1977. From left to right are Rosalynn Carter, the President, the Mayflower's Assistant General Manager Brad Jencks, and General Manager George DeKornfeld.

Vice-President Walter Mondale delivers a short speech in the East Room on inaugural night. Standing behind him are, left to right, Mrs. Mondale, Lynda Bird Robb, and Lucy Nugent (daughters of former President Johnson), Charles Robb, and Mrs. and Mr. Bardyl Tirana, head of the Inaugural Committee.

President Carter addressing the National Businessmen's Alliance at the hotel in December 1978.

Four years later, in 1981, it was good-bye to jeans and flannel shirts and hello to minks and limousines. Now it was the turn of the well-heeled who supported Ronald Reagan, and Reagan promised them a resurgence of solid American values and big dreams.

RESTORING THE GRANDE DAME

Near the end of the 1970s, the new owners of The Mayflower began to plan the physical reconstruction of the hotel. It had taken nearly ten years of thoughtful work to reach this stage. When the major restoration began in 1981, May-Wash Associates had already acquired a new partner—Stouffer Hotels. Under a twenty-year contract, Stouffer took over the management of the property from Westin Hotels, which had succeeded HCA in 1971 and had managed The Mayflower during the remainder of the decade. Stouffer decided to make The Mayflower the flagship of its growing hotel business. This decision was not without a personal element: The Stouffer Hotels president was now William Hulett, the man who had been general manager of The Mayflower in the 1970s, and who so graciously welcomed the Chinese delegation in 1973. He knew from direct experience what promise the hotel held, and what was needed to realize that promise.

The *Washington Post* summed it up well: "The Mayflower has a great opportunity to develop an identity, to become as great and enchanting a period piece of the 1920s as other hotels are of the 1890s. We hope the new managers understand this and that their modernization will not attempt to change The Mayflower into something it isn't."

The owners understood. And they went to work. They hired architects committed to the blending of new structural and design changes with the spirit and style of the 1920s hotel. The architects worked from old photographs, floor plans, and historic descriptions; the owners worked with the local landmarks committee and with Intradesigns, an interior-design firm headquartered in Los Angeles. The goal was twofold: to bring the hotel into the 1980s functionally while creating an aesthetic image faithful to the original conception. The goal was met and was immediately acknowledged by the nation's press. Typical of the observations was this report by Milly Wohler in the travel section of *The Oregonian*:

In 1982, The Mayflower Hotel had the patrician bone structure of a classic but aging beauty, important connections and a fascinating past. But there were a number of younger and flashier hotels in the nation's capital, and friends just weren't coming around as they once did. Today, $65 million later, the 60-year-old Mayflower has been restored physically and provides a complete new wardrobe, and it is busy charming a new generation of visitors.

Relatively little was done to the hotel's exterior, since the stately structure had been essentially unaltered over the years and was one of the architectural constants of the changing downtown Washington scene. A few modifications were made: The first-floor windows were enlarged and the doors replaced; and two floors were discreetly added to the 17th Street side of the building.

This 1985 photo, signed by President and Mrs. Ronald Reagan, was given to the hotel's general manager, Bernard Awenenti, at left. In the center are Mr. and Mrs. Richard Cohen.

Restoration of the interior was another matter; here significant changes were made. The hotel needed new restaurants, updated function rooms, remodeled guest rooms, and expanded kitchens. Under the supervision of Ulysses Auger (who, by this time, owned twenty-five restaurants), the kitchens were redesigned for more efficiency, and new equipment was installed to make the food-preparation facilities comparable to those of the best modern hotels. Also updated were the heating, plumbing, and electrical equipment. The passenger elevators were replaced by new walnut-finished cars with the latest elevator technology.

Equally significant were the interior's aesthetic changes. According to Gilbert A. Lewthwaite in the *Baltimore Sun*, ''The Mayflower, the grande dame of Washington hotels, shook her skirts yesterday and emerged from a three-year . . . facelift looking set for a new life of gracious living.''

Charles Lockwood, of *Skyline* magazine, observed:

. . . The architects returned the lobby to its 1925 splendour, complete with rose marble frieze, wall murals, and marble columns rising two stories to the richly embellished ceiling. By day, sunlight streams into the room through the skylights that were blacked out during World War II. By night, crystal chandeliers and custom-made torchères cast a soft glow that flatters the restored lobby and guests.

Other significant changes included reopening a second domed skylight in the Cafe Promenade, making the area (formerly The Mayflower Lounge) a cheerful, airy room for dining, and rediscovering and restoring the 1920s murals by Edward Laning. These were saved by partner Kingdon Gould, Jr., who caught the redecorators about to destroy them. ''They'd been around a long time and I was concerned with retaining the original look'', Gould recalls. He phoned New York

(top) *Workers rebuild the ceiling of the Grand Ballroom while a foreman studies the architectural plans for the restoration project, c. 1982.*

(bottom) *Restoring the 24 karat gold-leaf on one of the hotel's ornamental friezes. When first built, The Mayflower was said to have more gold-leaf than any other building in the country—except for the Library of Congress.*

art restorer Hiram H. Hoelzer, described the paintings, and asked, ''Do you know anything about a muralist called Edward Laning?'' Gould continued, ''It was like asking if Simon had ever heard of Garfunkel. Hoelzer came down to Washington, certified the murals as honest-to-goodness Lanings, and cleaned and varnished them.''

More changes: regilding all 24-karat-gold decorations throughout the public areas; refurbishing all 648 rooms and 76 suites, restoring the original 1925 fireplaces in the suites, adding Halian marble baths, and providing modern refrigerators; opening the Nicholas restaurant, which features fine dining in a décor of soft pink, beige, green, and white, and an adjoining dining room for intimate private parties; upgrading hotel services by adding a concierge, seven-day valet service, twenty-four-hour-valet parking, foreign currency exchange, international direct dialing, and a room directory printed in five languages.

In the course of the restoration, gold, silver, and cloisonné serving pieces, urns, vases, and candelabra were rescued from storage bins deep in the hotel cellars. The thirty-inch-tall urns were said to have belonged to actress Sarah Bernhardt.

A HISTORICAL LANDMARK AT LAST

The Mayflower was once again ready to entertain in its original, splendid style. The press and general public applauded the hotel's restoration: so did the National Park Service. On November 7, 1983, when the work was just about completed, the Service listed The Mayflower in the Register of Historical Places, certifying it as a National Landmark. The hotel received a written message from the President of the United States: ''Congratulations on this moment of historical importance for the community and our nation.'' He went on to note that ''as The Mayflower completes one of the most extensive private restoration projects undertaken in the District of Columbia, this special moment serves as a fitting tribute to a landmark of Washington.''

When The Mayflower formally reopened with a parade and gala party on November 20, 1984, Dominic Antonelli, Ulysses Auger, Richard Cohen, and Kingdon Gould, Jr., celebrated the high point of their business lives. In 1966, when the partners took the helm of The Mayflower, they committed themselves to putting the old hotel back on course. Seventeen years later, they had not only fulfilled their dream, but also received recognition for their accomplishment from the occupant of the White House—another landmark building with which The Mayflower has shared history-making for some sixty years.

Assembling crystal chandeliers during The Mayflower's restoration in 1982.

A ribbon-cutting ceremony was held on September 30, 1982. Shown here at the event are, left to right: co-owner Richard Cohen, son of William Cohen; co-owner Kingdon Gould, Jr.; Eric Ewolt, of Stouffer Hotels; and co-owner Ulysses Auger.

On November 20, 1984 a gala party celebrated completion of the hotel's restoration. From left to right: General Manager Bernard Awenenti; co-owners Kingdon Gould, Jr., Richard Cohen, and Ulysses Auger; and William Hulett, president of Stouffer Hotels and former Mayflower general manager.